中外文稀有版本文献

# 《德意志意识形态》

## ②

### 英文版

【德】卡尔·马克思　【德】弗里德里希·恩格斯 ◎ 著

中央编译出版社
Central Compilation & Translation Press

# 前　言

《德意志意识形态》全称《德意志意识形态。对费尔巴哈、布·鲍威尔和施蒂纳所代表的现代德国哲学以及各式各样先知所代表的德国社会主义的批判》，是马克思和恩格斯共同撰写的阐述唯物史观和共产主义理论的重要著作。这部著作共分为两卷，第一卷批评了路·费尔巴哈、布·鲍威尔、麦·施蒂纳的唯心史观，阐发了唯物史观的基本原理，论述了共产主义和无产阶级的革命的理论；第二卷批判了当时在德国流行的所谓"真正的社会主义"或"德国社会主义"，揭示了这种假社会主义的哲学基础、社会根源和阶级本质；该书揭示了人类社会发展的一般规律，论证了共产主义取代资本主义的历史必然性，提出了无产阶级夺取政权、消灭私有制、建设共产主义新社会的任务。

《德意志意识形态》是马克思和恩格斯于1845年至1846年共同完成的一部巨著，原文是德文。由于普鲁士官方书报检查机关的阻挠以及出版商对书中部分内容的担忧，这部著作在出版的道路上命运多舛，一直未能全部出版，仅仅第二卷的第四章在《威斯特伐利亚汽船》杂志1847年8月号和9月号上发表过。前苏共中央马克思列宁主义研究院于1932年首次全文用德文出版，1933年用俄文出版。

《德意志意识形态》第一卷第一章"费尔巴哈"是未完成的手稿。在手稿中，这一章原来的标题是"一、费尔巴哈"。马克思逝世后，恩格斯在整理其遗稿时，在手稿第一章的结尾处写有"一、费尔巴哈。唯物主义观点和唯心主义观点的对立"，很显然这是他对原有标题所作的具体说明。

由于《德意志意识形态》原文公开出版较迟，其传入中国的时间也较晚。1930年4月，上海亚东图书馆出版了程始仁编译的《辩证法经典》一书，含有《唯物的见解和唯心的见解之对立》一文，即《德意志意识形态》第一卷的摘译。1932年5月，上海昆仑书店出版了杨东莼、宁敦伍翻译的《费尔巴哈论》（又名《机械论的唯物论批判》）一书，含有《观念论的见解与唯物论的见解之对立》一文，即《德意志意识形态》第一卷摘译。1937年2月，南京《时事类编》第五卷第三期刊载荃麟翻译的《社会意识形态概说》一文，即《德意志意识形态》第一卷摘译。

1938年11月，上海言行出版社出版了郭沫若翻译的《德意志意识形态》一书，内容包括"马克思所著《德意志观念体系》序文之初稿"即"《德意志意识形态》第一卷序言"、"费尔巴哈——唯物论与唯心论的见解之对立"即《德意志意识形态》第一卷第一章"费尔巴哈。唯物主义观点和唯心主义观点的对立"的片断、"费尔巴哈论纲"，以及"译者弁言"和李亚山诺夫写的"编者导言"。1947年3月、1949年4月，该版本两次重印。1941年7月，上海珠林书店出版了克士（即周建人）翻译的《德意志观念体系》一书，即《德意志意识形态》第一卷的摘译。1948年8月，上海大用图书公司出版了周建人翻译的《新哲学手册》一书，将《德意志观念体系》一文收录其中。

中华人民共和国成立后，中央编译局翻译的《德意志意识形态》全新译本最早收录于1960年12月人民出版社出版的《马克思恩格斯全集》第三卷，1961年《德意志意识形态》单行本出版，此后市面流通的版本，基本为中央编译局译本。为进一步推动《德意志意识形态》的研究，中央编译出版社此次整理出版了《德意志意识形态》在全世界传播较为广泛的德文版、英文版（节选），以及1949年前中国出版的几个中文节译本，向国内学者提供权威的版本资料。如有不当之处，敬请批评指正。

张远航<br>2024年4月

**One of the classics of Marxian philosophy**

*A basic work on historical materialism*

# The GERMAN IDEOLOGY

## MARX & ENGELS

# THE
# GERMAN IDEOLOGY

# THE
# GERMAN IDEOLOGY

*PARTS I & III*

BY
KARL MARX
AND
FRIEDRICH ENGELS

*Edited with an Introduction by*
R. PASCAL

NEW YORK
INTERNATIONAL PUBLISHERS INC.

First Published - - - - - 1939

ALL RIGHTS RESERVED
1939
MADE AND PRINTED IN GREAT BRITAIN
PRINTED BY WESTERN PRINTING SERVICES LTD., (T.U. THROUGHOUT) BRISTOL

## CONTENTS

|  | PAGE |
|---|---|
| INTRODUCTION BY R. PASCAL | ix |
| PREFACE BY MARX | 1 |
| FEUERBACH. Opposition of the Materialistic and Idealistic Outlook | 3 |

   1. Ideology in General, German Ideology in Particular. . . . . . 4
      (*a*) History.
      (*b*) Concerning the Production of Consciousness.

   2. The Real Basis of Ideology. . . . 43
      (*a*) Intercourse and Productive Power.
      (*b*) Relation of State and Law to Property.
      (*c*) Natural and Civilized Instruments of Production and Forms of Property.

   3. Communism : The Production of the Form of Intercourse Itself. . . . . 70

TRUE SOCIALISM . . . . . . 79

   1. *The Rhenish Annals* or The Philosophy of True Socialism. . . . . . . 82
      (*a*) " Communism, Socialism, Humanism."
      (*b*) " Cornerstones of Socialism."

   2. Karl Grün—*The Social Movement in France and Belgium*, or *The Historiography of True Socialism*. . . . . . 118
      (*a*) Saint-Simonism.
      (*b*) Fourierism.
      (*c*) The " Limitations of Papa Cabet."
      (*d*) Proudhon.

CONTENTS

|   | PAGE |
|---|---|
| 3. Dr. Georg Kuhlmann of Holstein; or the Prophecies of True Socialism. | 180 |
| *APPENDIX*—THESES ON FEUERBACH | 195 |
| NOTES | 201 |
| INDEX OF AUTHORS | 209 |

## INTRODUCTION

*THE German Ideology*, the joint work of Marx and Engels, is their first and most comprehensive statement of historical materialism. Many of their smaller, separate articles of the years 1844 and 1845, and their earlier composite work, *The Holy Family*, foreshadow their later views; but this work, the product of a period of undisturbed co-operation, is almost completely free of idealistic traces of Hegel or Feuerbach. Despite the technical imperfectness of the text it is the first systematic account of their view of the relationship between the economic, political and intellectual activities of man, the first full statement of Marxism.

Both Marx and Engels were, at the outset of their careers, associated with the group of disciples of Hegel known as the Young Hegelians, the most prominent of whom were the publicist Arnold Ruge, the lecturer in theology Bruno Bauer, the schoolmaster Max Stirner, and the isolated figure of Ludwig Feuerbach. In the period of reaction in Prussia following the July revolution in France, these young men turned to criticism of the existing State and society. They had learnt from Hegel that the State is the embodiment of the Absolute Mind, of the ideas of Freedom, Justice, etc., and they demanded that it should really be so. They therefore subjected the dominant conceptions of their times to a detailed criticism, and maintained that if true notions were substituted for the prevailing ones, society would be reformed. Their first and most important work was, naturally enough, a criticism of religion. Feuerbach

INTRODUCTION

came to the notable conclusion that religion represents the inverted picture and imaginary satisfaction of the real interests of man, and called for a religion of man in place of God. His book, *The Essence of Christianity*,* exerted considerable influence not only in Germany.

Persecution followed on this openly expressed criticism —Bauer lost his post as lecturer at Bonn University— and the organ of this group, *The Halle Annals*, later *The German Annals*, adopted a more and more political tone. But while going to all lengths in " criticizing " existing conceptions and conventions, the characteristic of the group was that it refused to take part in movements of reform, believing that ideas lose their purity in the hands of the masses. This antithesis between intellect and the masses, established most paradoxically by Bauer, led soon to an antithesis between support of existing conditions and the movements of social reform, and many of this group ended up as ardent reactionaries. Feuerbach, by withdrawing from any active co-operation in political struggles, became abstract and ineffective in this philosophy; Stirner withdrew into an isolated verbal opposition of his own.

Only Marx and Engels accepted the challenge of the times. In 1842 Marx undertook the editorship of a newly founded radical newspaper, the *Rheinische Zeitung*. Here he came across the reality of the State in the form of the censorship, and found that the Prussian State, far from being an ideal form above classes, actively favoured the landed nobility against the peasantry and the proletariat. Forced to relinquish his post, he emigrated to Paris in November 1843, where a new world opened to him—a capitalist world in which there was an active working-class movement. He observed here how the backwardness of German conditions, i.e., the lack of a developed bourgeoisie and proletariat, was the cause of the in-

---

* Translated into English by George Eliot, 1854.

effectiveness of the Young-Hegelian revolt, and he threw himself into a study of the French Revolution of 1789 in order to elucidate the contemporary political situation. With Ruge he edited a publication, the *Deutsch-Französische Jahrbücher*, of which only one double-number appeared early in 1844. In two articles here, *On the Jewish Question* and *A Contribution to the Critique of the Hegelian Philosophy of Law*\* he expresses for the first time his communistic faith—a faith at this time, for he sees the proletariat essentially as the *means* for achieving " true " human relations, for solving the problems of philosophy. With the help of Feuerbach's *Provisional Theses towards the Reform of Philosophy*, of 1843, Marx had, however, gone a long way towards understanding the relationship between ideas and society. He attacks Bauer and his associates for being content to " proceed from the postulates of philosophy " (i.e. truth, freedom, justice, etc.) instead of criticizing existing social conditions. But he also believes that the modern German State can be analysed in its philosophy, since the latter, though illusory, is yet the " dream-history " of modern Germany. Hence he can write: " it is the philosopher in whose brain the revolution is beginning."

Engels had come to similar conclusions. He had been wrenched out of the abstract world of the Young Hegelians by a business journey to Manchester, and had there entered into relations with the working-class movement of Chartism. He threw himself enthusiastically into this real movement of emancipation, and was led thereby to examine the process of development of capitalism. At the same time as the above-mentioned articles of Marx, Engels too was writing that communism in Germany was the logical outcome of the Young-

---

\* Inaccurately translated in H. J. Stenning's *Selected Essays of Marx*, 1926.

INTRODUCTION

Hegelian philosophy, and that its most promising exponents were members of the educated class (article in *The New Moral World*, Nov. 1843). But Engels' practical experience led him further than Marx at this time. In two articles in the *Deutsch-Französische Jahrbücher* he analyses capitalism. In the article on Carlyle's *Past and Present*, while praising Carlyle's description of social conditions, he criticizes him for not seeing that these are the inevitable result of private property and that the socialist movement alone can abolish them; and in the important essay, *Sketch of a Critique of Political Economy*, he analyses the nature of private property, sketches its development to ever-growing monopoly, and the growth of its contradiction, the working class. In their conclusions Marx and Engels meet, but their modes of approach are complementary. In particular Marx was provided, by this essay of Engels, with the starting-point of his lifelong work on economics.

The two men recognized the kinship of their ideas, and in July 1844 their real friendship began with a visit of Engels to Marx in Paris. The first fruits of their co-operation, which was to be permanent and intimate, was *The Holy Family*, 1845, a criticism of the Young Hegelians in the light of the revolutionary movement and revolutionary theory elsewhere. The detailed analysis and refutation of writers like Bruno and Edgar Bauer, Szeliga, etc., is of little general interest to-day, but it is of great significance as showing the thoroughness with which Marx laid the foundations of his social theories. Repeatedly he makes generalizations which open up the vista of his life's work. The following passage is an example:

'Proletariat and Wealth are opposites. As such they form a whole. They are both formations of the world of private property. What concerns us here is to define the particular position they take within the opposition. It is not enough to state that they are two sides of a whole.

'Private property as private property, as wealth, is forced to maintain its own existence and thereby the existence of its opposite, the proletariat. It is the positive side of the opposition, private property satisfied in itself.

'*Vice versa*, the proletariat is, as proletariat, forced to abolish itself and, with this, the opposite which determines it, which makes it the proletariat, private property. It is the negative side of the opposition, its principle of unrest, private property which is dissolved and in process of dissolution. . . .

'Within the opposition, therefore, the owner of private property is the conservative, the proletarian the destructive party. From the former derives the action of preservation of the opposition, from the latter the action of its destruction.

'Of course, in its economic movement private property drives on to its own dissolution, but only by a development which is independent of and opposed to its will, unconscious, conditioned by the nature of the matter; i.e. by the production of the proletariat *as* proletariat, of poverty which is conscious of its intellectual and bodily poverty, of loss of humanity, conscious of itself and therefore abolishing itself. The proletariat carries out the verdict which private property pronounces on itself by the very production of the proletariat, just as it carries out the verdict which wage-labour pronounces on itself by producing the wealth of others and its own poverty. If the proletariat is victorious it does not at all mean that it has become the absolute side of society, for it is victorious only by abolishing itself and its opposite. Then both the proletariat and its conditioning opposite, private property, have vanished.' (Chap. 4).

Few passages show so clearly how Marx's study of society and socialist writings (the passage is part of a commentary on Proudhon) was impregnated with the dialectic he had learnt from Hegel. Precisely from the dialectic he was prepared to see the true relations of private property and the proletariat, and to see, as against Proudhon, what conditions were involved in the abolition of private property.

The main part of *The Holy Family* was Marx's work. Meanwhile Engels, back in England, was working at his *Condition of the Working Class in England in 1844* which appeared later in 1845.\* This work is significant not only for its description of the conditions of the working class. It is also an analysis of the mode of development of the bourgeoisie and the capitalist mode of production, hence an analysis of the development of the proletariat and of the class struggle. It is a concrete elaboration of the theses contained in the above-quoted passage of Marx from *The Holy Family* and follows the same dialectical method. Mehring has rightly called it "one of the foundation stones of socialism."

In the spring of 1845 Engels joined Marx in the latter's exile in Brussels, and there now began the period of their closest co-operation. Both studied intensely the history of capitalism, the writings of political economists and socialists. In the summer they made a visit to England, where Marx was introduced to the leaders of Chartism and devoured the works of English economists.

*The German Ideology* is the outcome of this period. Completed by the summer of 1846, it contains under the form of a last reckoning with Feuerbach, Stirner, and the "true socialists" a positive statement of their own interpretation of the world.

Only the last section of *The German Ideology* was published during the lifetime of Marx and Engels,

\* Translated into English, 1892.

owing to the reluctance of German publishers. The text is, particularly in the first section, *Feuerbach*, sometimes imperfect, and further impaired by " the gnawing criticism of the mice." Very comprehensive in its scope, the work must not be considered as expressing the final opinions of Marx and Engels. In the Preface to his later work on Feuerbach,* Engels says of *The Ideology*:

'The part of it dealing with Feuerbach is not complete. The portion finished consists of an exposition of the materialistic view of history, and only proves how incomplete at that time was our knowledge of economic history.'

Again, in a letter to Mehring, 14th July 1893, Engels wrote of the joint early works:

'We all laid and were bound to lay the main emphasis at first on the derivation of political, juridical and other ideological notions, and of the actions arising through the medium of these notions, from basic economic facts. But in doing so we neglected the formal side—the way in which these notions came about—for the sake of the content.'

In spite of these shortcomings it will be found that *The Ideology* offers a wealth of idea in its interpretation of history which can hardly be found elsewhere.

It is divided into three main Parts: (1) Feuerbach; (2) The Leipzig Concilium (Bruno Bauer and Max Stirner); (3) True Socialism. The whole occupies 528 of the big pages of the *Marx-Engels Gesamtausgabe*, and it has been considered advisable to omit the whole of the second Part (pp. 71–432). In this way it has been possible to produce a small and inexpensive book which contains the gist of *The Ideology* in the most accessible form.

The first section, Feuerbach, is in no way a detailed

* *Ludwig Feuerbach and the Outcome of Classical German Philosophy*, 1886. English translation, 1934.

criticism of Feuerbach.* It sets out the authors' approach to the problems of philosophy in positive form, beginning with the conditions of all thought and all history, and serves as a general introduction:

> 'The premises from which we begin are not arbitrary ones, not dogmas, but real . . . the real individuals, their activity, and the material conditions determining their life.'

They sketch the development of human society which is essentially a history of " material production " through the division of labour, i.e., of the growth of private property; they examine the relations between economic forces and political, juridical, theoretical forms; and finally give an outline of human relations in communist society. Many of the ideas and formulations occur in similar form in the later works, in *The Communist Manifesto*, *A Critique of Political Economy*, *Capital*, *Anti-Dühring*, etc.

The second section is entirely different in method. After a final blow at Bruno Bauer, the authors enter on an extremely detailed examination of Max Stirner's bulky book, *Der Einzige und sein Eigentum*, 1845,† in which they do not restrain their exuberance. Stirner is of some consequence himself, being recognized by anarchists as one of the first anarchist writers. The method Marx and Engels adopted in treating his work is not, however, easy to follow. Since Stirner, in his definition of man, considers each as " unique " and calls on men to cut themselves free of all assumptions, historical and moral, Marx and Engels call him a " saint " and invent a framework in which " Saints " Bruno (Bauer) and Max (Stirner) sit in judgment on the heretic

---

* A few pages of the first section have appeared in translation in Emile Burns' *A Handbook of Marxism*, 1935.

† Translated into English by Byington as *The Ego and his Own*, 1912.

INTRODUCTION  xvii

Feuerbach. Unfortunately this apt conception is cut across by other analogies. For long periods the authors refer to Stirner as Sancho Panza, or "Jacques le bonhomme"; they drop into his own way of talking to satirize him, and hilariously parody him. But continually, in this exuberant extravaganza, brilliant generalizations are made whose absence from this volume can only be regretted.

The third section deals with a group of writers known as "true socialists." These men, Grün, Lüning, Püttmann, Kuhlmann, Hess (though the last came round to the point of view of Marx and Engels) were not opponents of socialist theory, like Bauer and Stirner; but, as Marx says in *The Communist Manifesto*, they adapted the theories of the French socialists, Fourier, Cabet and others, to the needs of the German petty bourgeoisie, turning from the real working-class movement to ideal solutions in terms of traditional German philosophy. They were influential in the years 1845–1848 through a number of periodicals (the *Gesellschaftsspiegel*, the *Rheinische Jahrbücher*, the *Deutsches Bürgerbuch*, and the *Westfälisches Dampfboot*, and played a part on the left wing of the revolutionary movement of 1848. Their confused and feeble theories are typical of the backward, semi-proletarian petty-bourgeoisie, but find many echoes in the outlook which has dominated at times the socialist movement in advanced countries.

*The German Ideology* was first published in full in 1932, in the edition of the Marx-Engels-Lenin Institute, in Moscow, the *Marx-Engels Gesamtausgabe* I, 5; and in the edition of Landshut and Mayer, *Marx, Der Historische Materialismus*, in somewhat different arrangement. I have followed the *Gesamtausgabe* and am indebted to the magnificent critical notes. I have appended a translation of the original *Theses on Feuerbach* of Marx, first published in their original form in the two above-

B

## INTRODUCTION

mentioned editions. They show enough divergence from the edition popularized by Engels to make study of them worth while.

Practically all the bibliographical material in the Notes* and Index comes from the *Gesamtausgabe*; explanatory notes are my own.

R. PASCAL.

---

*The Notes appear on pp. 201–7, and are numbered consecutively in each section.

# THE GERMAN IDEOLOGY

## PREFACE

HITHERTO men have constantly made up for themselves false conceptions about themselves, about what they are and what they ought to be. They have arranged their relationships according to their ideas of God, of normal man, etc. The phantoms of their brains have gained the mastery over them. They, the creators, have bowed down before their creatures. Let us liberate them from the chimeras, the ideas, dogmas, imaginary beings under the yoke of which they are pining away. Let us revolt against the rule of thoughts. Let us teach men, says one,[1] to exchange these imaginations for thoughts which correspond to the essence of man; says the second,[2] to take up a critical attitude to them; says the third,[3] to knock them out of their heads; and—existing reality will collapse.

These innocent and childlike fancies are the kernel of the modern Young-Hegelian philosophy, which not only is received by the German public with horror and awe, but is announced by our philosophic Heroes with the solemn consciousness of their cataclysmic dangerousness and criminal ruthlessness. The first volume of this present publication has the aim of uncloaking these sheep, who take themselves and are taken for wolves; of showing how their bleating merely imitates in a philosophic form the conceptions of the German middle class; how the boasting of these philosophic commentators only mirrors the wretchedness of the real conditions in Germany. It is its aim to discredit the philosophic struggle with the shadows of reality, which appeals to the dreamy and muddled German nation.

Once upon a time an honest fellow had the idea that men were drowned in water only because they were possessed with the idea of gravity. If they were to knock this idea out of their heads, say by stating it to be a superstition, a religious idea, they would be sublimely proof against any danger from water. His whole life long he fought against the illusion of gravity, of whose harmful results all statistics brought him new and manifold evidence. This honest fellow was the type of the new revolutionary philosophers in Germany.

KARL MARX.

# FEUERBACH
## Opposition of the Materialistic and Idealistic Outlook

As we hear from German ideologists, Germany has in the last few years gone through an unparalleled revolution. The decomposition of the Hegelian philosophy, which began with Strauss, has developed into a universal ferment into which all the " powers of the past " are swept. In the general chaos mighty empires have arisen only to meet with immediate doom, heroes have emerged momentarily only to be hurled into obscurity by bolder and stronger rivals. It was a revolution beside which the French Revolution was child's play, a world struggle beside which the struggles of the Diadochi[4] appear insignificant. Principles ousted one another, heroes of the mind overthrew each other with unheard-of rapidity, and in the three years 1842–1845 more of the past was swept away than normally in three centuries.

All this is supposed to have taken place in the realm of pure thought.

Certainly it is an interesting event we are dealing with: the putrescence of the absolute spirit. When the last spark of its life had failed, the various components of this *caput mortuum*[5] began to decompose, entered on new combinations and formed new substances. The industrialists of philosophy, who till then had lived on the exploitation of the absolute spirit, now seized upon the new combinations. Each with all possible zeal set about retailing his apportioned share. This naturally gave rise to competition, which, to start with, was carried on in moderately staid bourgeois fashion. Later when the German market was glutted, and the commodity in

3

spite of all efforts found no response in the world-market, the business was spoiled in the usual German manner by fake and shoddy production, deterioration in quality, adulteration of the raw materials, falsification of labels, fake purchases, bill-jobbing and a credit-system devoid of any real basis. The competition turned into a bitter struggle, which is now being extolled and interpreted to us as a revolution of world significance, the begetter of the most prodigious results and achievements.

If we wish to rate at its true value this philosophic charlatanry, which awakens even in the breast of the honest German citizen a glow of national pride, if we wish to bring out clearly the pettiness, the parochial narrowness of this whole Young-Hegelian movement and the tragi-comic contrast between the illusions of these heroes about their achievements and the actual achievements themselves, we must look at the whole spectacle from a standpoint beyond the frontiers of Germany.

## 1. IDEOLOGY IN GENERAL, GERMAN IDEOLOGY IN PARTICULAR.

German criticism has, right up to its latest efforts, never quitted the realm of philosophy. Far from examining its general philosophic premises,[6] the whole body of its inquiries has actually sprung from the soil of a definite philosophical system, that of Hegel. Not only in their answers but in their very questions there was a mystification. This dependence on Hegel is the reason why not one of these modern critics has even attempted a comprehensive criticism of the Hegelian system, however much each professes to have advanced beyond Hegel. Their polemics against Hegel and against one another are confined to this—each extracts one side of the Hegelian system and turns this against the whole system as well as against the sides extracted by the others. To begin with they extracted pure unfalsified Hegelian categories such as "substance" and "self-consciousness," later they desecrated these categories with more secular names such as "species," "the unique," "man," etc.

The entire body of German philosophical criticism from Strauss to Stirner is confined to criticism of religious conceptions. The critics started from real religion and actual theology. What religious consciousness and a religious conception really meant was determined variously as they went along. Their advance consisted in subsuming[7] the allegedly dominant metaphysical, political, juridical, moral and other conceptions under the class of religious or theological conceptions; and similarly in pronouncing political, juridical, moral consciousness as religious or theological, and the political, juridical, moral man—"man" in the last resort—as religious. The dominance of religion was taken for granted. Gradually every dominant relationship was pronounced a religious relationship and transformed into a cult, a cult of law, cult of the State, etc. On all sides it was only a question of dogmas and belief in dogmas. The world was sanctified to an ever-increasing extent till at last our venerable Saint Max[8] was able to canonize it *en bloc* and thus dispose of it once for all.

The Old Hegelians had *comprehended* everything as soon as it was reduced to an Hegelian logical category. The Young Hegelians *criticized* everything by attributing to it religious conceptions or by pronouncing it a theological matter. The Young Hegelians are in agreement with the Old Hegelians in their belief in the rule of religion, of concepts, of an abstract general principle in the existing world. Only, the one party attacks this dominion as usurpation, while the other extols it as legitimate.

Since the Young Hegelians consider conceptions, thoughts, ideas, in fact all the products of consciousness, to which they attribute an independent existence, as the real chains of men (just as the Old Hegelians declared them the true bonds of human society) it is evident that the Young Hegelians have to fight only against these illusions of the consciousness. Since, according to their fantasy, the relationships of men, all their doings, their chains and their limitations are products of their consciousness, the Young Hegelians logically put to men the moral postulate of exchanging their present consciousness for human, critical or egoistic consciousness, and thus of removing their limitations.⁹ This demand to change consciousness amounts to a demand to interpret reality in another way, i.e. to accept it by means of another interpretation. The Young-Hegelian ideologists, in spite of their allegedly " world-shattering " statements, are the staunchest conservatives. The most recent of them have found the correct expression for their activity when they declare they are only fighting against " phrases." They forget, however, that to these phrases they themselves are only opposing other phrases, and that they are in no way combating the real existing world when they are merely combating the phrases of this world. The only results which this philosophic criticism could achieve were a few (and at that thoroughly one-sided) elucidations of Christianity from the point of view of religious history ; all the rest of their assertions are only further embellishments of their claim to have furnished, in these unimportant elucidations, discoveries of universal importance.

It has not occurred to any one of these philosophers to inquire into the connection of German philosophy with German reality, the relation of their criticism to their own material surroundings.

. . . . .

The premises from which we begin are not arbitrary ones, not dogmas, but real premises from which abstraction can only be made in the imagination. They are the real individuals, their activity and the material conditions under which they live, both those which they find already existing and those produced by their activity. These premises can thus be verified in a purely empirical way.

The first premise of all human history is, of course, the existence of living human individuals. Thus the first fact to be established is the physical organization of these individuals and their consequent relation to the rest of nature. Of course, we cannot here go either into the actual physical nature of man, or into the natural conditions in which man finds himself—geological, orohydrographical, climatic and so on. The writing of history must always set out from these natural bases and their modification in the course of history through the action of man.

Men can be distinguished from animals by consciousness, by religion or anything else you like. They themselves begin to distinguish themselves from animals as soon as they begin to *produce* their means of subsistence, a step which is conditioned by their physical organization. By producing their means of subsistence men are indirectly producing their actual material life.

The way in which men produce their means of subsistence depends first of all on the nature of the actual means they find in existence and have to reproduce. This mode of production must not be considered simply as being the reproduction of the physical existence of the individuals. Rather it is a definite form of activity of these individuals, a definite form of expressing their life, a definite *mode of life* on their part. As individuals express their life, so they are. What they are, therefore, coincides with their production, both with *what* they produce and with *how* they produce. The nature of individuals thus depends on the material conditions determining their production.

This production only makes its appearance with the increase of population. In its turn this presupposes the intercourse of individuals with one another. The form of this intercourse is again determined by production.

The relations of different nations among themselves depend upon the extent to which each has developed its productive forces, the division of labour and internal intercourse.[10] This statement is generally recognized. But not only the relation of one nation to others, but also the whole internal structure of the nation itself depends on the stage of development reached by its production and its internal and external intercourse. How far the productive forces of a nation are developed is shown most manifestly by the degree to which the division of labour has been carried. Each new productive force, in so far as it is not merely a quantitative extension of productive forces already known, (for instance the bringing into cultivation of fresh land), brings about a further development of the division of labour.

The division of labour inside a nation leads at first to the separation of industrial and commercial from agricultural labour, and hence to the separation of town and country and a clash of interests between them. Its further development leads to the separation of commercial from industrial labour. At the same time through the division of labour there develop further, inside these various branches, various divisions among the individuals co-operating in definite kinds of labour. The relative position of these individual groups is determined by the methods employed in agriculture, industry and commerce (patriarchalism, slavery, estates, classes). These same conditions are to be seen (given a more developed intercourse) in the relations of different nations to one another.

The various stages of development in the division of labour are just so many different forms of ownership; i.e. the existing stage in the division of labour determines also the relations of individuals to one another with reference to the material, instrument, and product of labour.

The first form of ownership is tribal ownership. It corresponds to the undeveloped stage of production, at which a people lives by hunting and fishing, by the rearing of beasts or, in the highest stage, agriculture. In the latter case it presupposes a great mass of uncultivated stretches of land. The division of labour is at this stage still very elementary and is confined to a further extension of the natural division of labour imposed by the family. The social structure is therefore limited to an extension of the family; patriarchal family chieftains; below them the members of the tribe; finally slaves. The slavery latent in the family only develops gradually with the increase of population, the growth of wants, and with the extension of external relations, of war or of trade.

The second form is the ancient communal and State ownership which proceeds especially from the union of several tribes into a city by agreement or by conquest, and which is still accompanied by slavery. Beside communal ownership we already find movable, and later also immovable, private property developing,[11] but as an abnormal form subordinate to communal ownership. It is only as a community that the citizens hold power over their labouring slaves, and on this account alone, therefore, they are bound to the form of communal ownership. It is the communal private property which compels the active citizens to remain in this natural[12] form of association over against their slaves. For this reason the whole structure of society based on this communal ownership, and with it the power of the people, decays in the same measure as immovable private property evolves. The division of labour is already more developed. We already find the antagonism of town and country; later the antagonism between those states which represent town interests and those which represent country, and inside the towns themselves the antagonism between industry and maritime commerce. The class relation between citizens and slaves is now completely developed.

This whole interpretation of history appears to be contradicted by the fact of conquest. Up till now violence, war, pillage, rape and slaughter, etc. have been accepted as the driving force of history. Here we must limit ourselves to the chief points and take therefore only a striking example—the destruction of an old civilization by a barbarous people and the resulting formation of an entirely new organization of society. (Rome and the barbarians; Feudalism and Gaul; the Byzantine Empire and the Turks). With the conquering barbarian people war itself is still, as hinted above, a regular form of intercourse, which is the more eagerly exploited as the population increases, involving the necessity of new means of production to supersede the traditional and, for it, the only possible, crude mode of production. In Italy it was, however, otherwise. The concentration of landed property (caused not only by buying-up and indebtedness but also by inheritance, since loose living being rife and marriage rare, the old families died out and their possessions fell into the hands of a few) and its conversion into grazing-land (caused not only by economic forces still operative to-day but by the importation of plundered and tribute-corn and the resultant lack of demand for Italian corn) brought about the almost total disappearance of the free population. The very slaves died out again and again, and had constantly to be replaced by new ones. Slavery remained the basis of the whole productive system. The plebeians, mid-way between freemen and slaves, never succeeded in becoming more than a proletarian rabble. Rome indeed never became more than a city; its connection with the provinces was almost exclusively political and could therefore easily be broken again by political events.

With the development of private property, we find here for the first time the same conditions which we shall find again, only on a more extensive scale, with modern private property. On the one hand the concentration of private property, which began very early in Rome, (as the Licinian agrarian law proves[13]), and proceeded very rapidly from the time of the civil wars and especially under the Emperors; on the other hand, coupled with this, the transformation of the plebeian small peasantry into a proletariat, which, however, owing to its intermediate position between propertied citizens and slaves, never achieved an independent development.

The third form of ownership is feudal or estate-property.[14] If antiquity started out from the town and its little territory, the Middle Ages started out from the country. This different starting-point was determined by the sparseness of the population at that time, which was scattered over a large area and which received no large increase from the conquerors. In contrast to Greece and Rome, feudal development therefore extends over a much wider field, prepared by the Roman conquests and the spread of agriculture at first associated with it. The last centuries of the declining Roman Empire and its conquest by the barbarians destroyed a number of productive forces; agriculture had declined, industry had decayed for want of a market, trade had died out or been violently suspended, the rural and urban population had decreased. From these conditions and the mode of organization of the conquest determined by them, feudal property developed under the influence of the Germanic military constitution. Like tribal and communal ownership, it is based again on a community; but the directly producing class standing over against it is not, as in the case of the ancient community, the slaves, but the enserfed small peasantry. As soon as feudalism is fully developed, there also arises antagonism to the towns. The hierarchical system of land ownership, and the armed bodies of retainers associated with it, gave the nobility power over the serfs. This feudal organization was, just as much as the ancient communal ownership, an association against a subjected producing class; but the form of association and the relation to the direct producers were different because of the different conditions of production.

This feudal organization of land-ownership had its counterpart in the towns in the shape of corporative property, the feudal organization of trades. Here property consisted chiefly in the labour of each individual person. The necessity for association against the organized robber-nobility, the need for communal covered markets in an age when the industrialist was at the same time a merchant, the growing competition of the escaped serfs swarming into the rising towns, the feudal structure of the whole country : these combined to bring about the guilds. Further, the gradually accumulated capital of individual craftsmen and their stable numbers, as against the growing population, evolved the relation of journeyman and apprentice, which brought into being in the towns a hierarchy similar to that in the country.

Thus the chief form of property during the feudal epoch consisted on the one hand of landed property with serf-labour chained to it, and on the other of individual labour with small capital commanding the labour of journeymen. The organization of both was determined

## FEUERBACH

by the restricted conditions of production—the small-scale and primitive cultivation of the land, and the craft type of industry. There was little division of labour in the heyday of feudalism. Each land bore in itself the conflict of town and country and the division into estates was certainly strongly marked; but apart from the differentiation of princes, nobility, clergy and peasants in the country, and masters, journeymen, apprentices and soon also the rabble of casual labourers in the towns, no division of importance took place. In agriculture it was rendered difficult by the strip-system, beside which the cottage industry of the peasants themselves emerged as another factor. In industry there was no division of labour at all in the individual trades themselves, and very little between them. The separation of industry and commerce was found already in existence in older towns; in the newer it only developed later, when the towns entered into mutual relations.

The grouping of larger territories into feudal kingdoms was a necessity for the landed nobility as for the towns. The organization of the ruling class, the nobility, had, therefore, everywhere a monarch at its head.

The fact is, therefore, that definite individuals who are productively active in a definite way enter into these definite social and political relations. Empirical observation must in each separate instance bring out empirically, and without any mystification and speculation, the connection of the social and political structure with production. The social structure and the State are continually evolving out of the life-process of definite individuals, but of individuals, not as they may appear in their own or other people's imagination, but as they really are; i.e. as they are effective, produce materially, and are active under definite material limits, presuppositions and conditions independent of their will.

The production of ideas, of conceptions, of consciousness, is at first directly interwoven with the material activity and the material intercourse of men, the language of real life. Conceiving, thinking, the mental intercourse of men, appear at this stage as the direct efflux of their material behaviour. The same applies to mental production as expressed in the language of the politics, laws, morality, religion, metaphysics of a people. Men are the producers of their conceptions, ideas, etc.— real, active men, as they are conditioned by a definite development of their productive forces and of the intercourse corresponding to these, up to its furthest forms. Consciousness can never be anything else than conscious existence, and the existence of men is their actual life-process. If in all ideology men and their circumstances appear upside down as in a *camera obscura*,[15] this phenomenon arises just as much from their historical life-process as the inversion of objects on the retina does from their physical life-process.

In direct contrast to German philosophy which descends from heaven to earth, here we ascend from earth to heaven. That is to say, we do not set out from what men say, imagine, conceive, nor from men as narrated, thought of, imagined, conceived, in order to arrive at men in the flesh. We set out from real, active men, and on the basis of their real life-process we demonstrate the development of the ideological reflexes and echoes of this life-process. The phantoms formed in the human brain are also, necessarily, sublimates of their material life-process, which is empirically verifiable and bound to material premises. Morality, religion, metaphysics, all the rest of ideology and their corresponding forms of consciousness, thus no longer retain the semblance of independence. They have no history, no development; but men, developing their material production and their material intercourse, alter, along with this their real existence, their thinking and the products of their thinking. Life is not determined by consciousness, but consciousness by life. In the first method of approach the starting-point is consciousness taken as the living individual; in the second it is the real living individuals themselves, as they are in actual life, and consciousness is considered solely as *their* consciousness.

This method of approach is not devoid of premises. It starts out from the real premises and does not abandon them for a moment. Its premises are men, not in any fantastic isolation or abstract definition, but in their actual, empirically perceptible process of development under definite conditions. As soon as this active life-process is described, history ceases to be a collection of dead facts as it is with the empiricists (themselves still abstract), or an imagined activity of imagined subjects, as with the idealists.

Where speculation ends—in real life—there real, positive science begins: the representation of the practical activity, of the practical process of development of men. Empty talk about consciousness ceases, and real knowledge has to take its place. When reality is depicted, philosophy as an independent branch of activity loses its medium of existence. At the best its place can only be taken by a summing-up of the most general results, abstractions which arise from the observation of the historical development of men. Viewed apart from real history, these abstractions have in themselves no value whatsoever. They can only serve to facilitate the arrangement of historical material, to indicate the sequence of its separate strata. But they by no means afford a recipe or schema, as does philosophy, for neatly trimming the epochs of history. On the contrary, our difficulties begin only when we set about the observation and the arrangement—the real depiction—of our historical material, whether of a past epoch or of the present. The removal of these difficulties is governed by premises which it is quite impossible to state here, but which only the study of the actual life-process and the activity of the individuals of each epoch will make evident. We shall select here some of these abstractions, which we use to refute the ideologists, and shall illustrate them by historical examples.

## (a) *History.*

Since we are dealing with the Germans, who do not postulate anything, we must begin by stating the first premise of all human existence, and therefore of all history, the premise namely that men must be in a position to live in order to be able to " make history." But life involves before everything else eating and drinking, a habitation, clothing and many other things. The first historical act is thus the production of the means to satisfy these needs, the production of material life itself. And indeed this is an historical act, a fundamental condition of all history, which to-day, as thousands of years ago, must daily and hourly be fulfilled merely in order to sustain human life. Even when the sensuous world is reduced to a minimum, to a stick as with Saint Bruno,[16] it presupposes the action of producing the stick. The first necessity therefore in any theory of history is to observe this fundamental fact in all its significance and all its implications and to accord it its due importance. This, as is notorious, the Germans have never done, and they have never therefore had an earthly basis for history and consequently never a historian. The French and the English, even if they have conceived the relation of this fact with so-called history only in an extremely one-sided fashion, particularly as long as they remained in the toils of political ideology, have nevertheless made the first attempts to give the writing of history a materialistic basis by being the first to write histories of civil society, of commerce and industry.

The second fundamental point is that as soon as a need

is satisfied, (which implies the action of satisfying, and the acquisition of an instrument), new needs are made; and this production of new needs is the first historical act. Here we recognize immediately the spiritual ancestry of the great historical wisdom of the Germans who, when they run out of positive material and when they can serve up neither theological nor political nor literary rubbish, do not write history at all, but invent the "prehistoric era." They do not, however, enlighten us as to how we proceed from this nonsensical "prehistory" to history proper; although, on the other hand, in their historical speculation they seize upon this "prehistory" with especial eagerness because they imagine themselves safe there from interference on the part of "crude facts," and, at the same time, because there they can give full rein to their speculative impulse and set up and knock down hypotheses by the thousand.

The third circumstance which, from the very first, enters into historical development, is that men, who daily remake their own life, begin to make other men, to propagate their kind: the relation between man and wife, parents and children, the FAMILY. The family which to begin with is the only social relationship, becomes later, when increased needs create new social relations and the increased population new needs, a subordinate one (except in Germany), and must then be treated and analysed according to the existing empirical data*, not according to "the concept of the family," as is the custom in Germany. These three aspects of social activity are

* The building of houses. With savages each family has of course its own cave or hut like the separate family tent of the nomads. This separate domestic economy is made only the more necessary by the further development of private property. With the agricultural peoples a communal domestic economy is just as impossible as a communal cultivation of the soil. A great advance was the building of towns. In all previous periods, however, the abolition of individual economy, which is inseparable from the abolition of private property, was impossible for the simple reason that the material conditions governing it were not present. The setting-up of a communal domestic economy presupposes the development of machinery, of the use of natural forces and of many other productive forces—e.g. of water-supplies, of

not of course to be taken as three different stages, but just, as I have said, as three aspects or, to make it clear to the Germans, three " moments,"[17] which have existed simultaneously since the dawn of history and the first men, and still assert themselves in history to-day.

The production of life, both of one's own in labour and of fresh life in procreation, now appears as a double relationship : on the one hand as a natural, on the other as a social relationship. By social we understand the co-operation of several individuals, no matter under what conditions, in what manner and to what end. It follows from this that a certain mode of production, or industrial stage, is always combined with a certain mode of co-operation, or social stage, and this mode of co-operation is itself a " productive force." Further, that the multitude of productive forces accessible to men determines the nature of society, hence that the " history of humanity " must always be studied and treated in relation to the history of industry and exchange. But it is also clear how in Germany it is impossible to write this sort of history, because the Germans lack not only the necessary power of comprehension and the material but also the " evidence of their senses," for across the Rhine you cannot have any experience of these things since history has stopped happening. Thus it is quite obvious from the start that there exists a materialistic connection of men with one another, which is determined by their needs and their mode of production, and which is as old as men themselves. This con-

---

gas-lighting, steam-heating, etc., the removal of the antagonism of town and country. Without these conditions a communal economy would not in itself form a new productive force ; lacking any material basis and resting on a purely theoretical foundation, it would be a mere freak and would end in nothing more than a monastic economy.— What was possible can be seen in the formation of towns and the erection of communal buildings for various definite purposes (prisons, barracks, etc.). That the abolition of individual economy is inseparable from the abolition of the family is self-evident.

nection is ever taking on new forms, and thus presents a "history" independently of the existence of any political or religious nonsense which would hold men together on its own.

Only now, after having considered four moments, four aspects of the fundamental historical relationships, do we find that man also possesses "consciousness"; but, even so, not inherent, not "pure" consciousness. From the start the "spirit" is afflicted with the curse of being "burdened" with matter, which here makes its appearance in the form of agitated layers of air, sounds, in short of language. Language is as old as consciousness, language is practical consciousness, as it exists for other men, and for that reason is really beginning to exist for me personally as well; for language, like consciousness, only arises from the need, the necessity, of intercourse with other men. Where there exists a relationship, it exists for me: the animal has no "relations" with anything, cannot have any. For the animal, its relation to others does not exist as a relation. Consciousness is therefore from the very beginning a social product, and remains so as long as men exist at all. Consciousness is at first, of course, merely consciousness concerning the immediate sensuous environment and consciousness of the limited connection with other persons and things outside the individual who is growing self-conscious. At the same time it is consciousness of nature, which first appears to men as a completely alien, all-powerful and unassailable force, with which men's relations are purely animal and by which they are overawed like beasts; it is thus a purely animal consciousness of nature (natural religion).

We see here immediately: this natural religion or animal behaviour towards nature is determined by the form of society and *vice versa*. Here, as everywhere, the identity of nature and man appears in such a way that the restricted relation of men to nature determines their restricted relation to one another, and their restricted relation to one another determines men's restricted relation to nature, just because nature is as yet hardly modified historically; and, on the other hand, man's consciousness of the necessity of associating with the individuals around him is the beginning of the consciousness that he is living in society at all. This beginning is as animal as social life itself at this stage. It is mere herd-consciousness, and at this point man is only distinguished from sheep by the fact that with him consciousness takes the place of instinct or that his instinct is a conscious one.

This sheep-like or tribal consciousness receives its further development and extension through increased productivity, the increase of needs, and, what is fundamental to both of these, the increase of population. With these there develops the division of labour, which was originally nothing but the division of labour in the sexual act, then that division of labour which develops spontaneously or "naturally"[18] by virtue of natural predisposition (e.g. physical strength), needs, accidents, etc., etc. Division of labour only becomes truly such from the moment when a division of material and mental labour appears. From this moment onwards consciousness *can* really flatter itself that it is something other than consciousness of existing practice, that it is *really* conceiving something without conceiving something *real*; from now on consciousness is in a position to emancipate itself from the world and to proceed to the formation of "pure" theory, theology, philosophy, ethics, etc. But even if this theory, theology, philosophy, ethics, etc. comes into contradiction with the existing relations, this can only occur as a result of the fact that existing social relations have come into contradiction with existing forces of production; this, moreover, can also occur in a particular national sphere of relations through the appearance of the contradiction, not within the national orbit, but between this national consciousness and the practice of other nations, i.e. between the national and the general consciousness of a nation.

Moreover, it is quite immaterial what consciousness starts to do on its own: out of all such muck we get only the one inference that these three moments, the forces of production, the state of society, and consciousness, can and must come into contradiction with one another, because the division of labour implies the possibility, nay the fact that intellectual and material activity—enjoyment and labour, production and consumption—devolve on different individuals, and that the only possibility of their not coming into contradiction lies in the negation in its turn of the division of labour. It is self-evident, moreover, that " spectres," " bonds," " the higher being," " concept," " scruple," are merely the idealistic, spiritual expression, the conception apparently of the isolated individual, the image of very empirical fetters and limitations, within which the mode of production of life, and the form of intercourse coupled with it, move.

With the division of labour, in which all these contradictions are implicit, and which in its turn is based on the natural division of labour in the family and the separation of society into individual families opposed to one another, is given simultaneously the distribution, and indeed the unequal distribution, (both quantitative and qualitative), of labour and its products, hence property: the nucleus, the first form, of which lies in the family, where wife and children are the slaves of the husband. This latent slavery in the family, though still very crude, is the first property, but even at this early stage it corresponds perfectly to the definition of modern economists who call it the power of disposing of the labour-power of others. Division of labour and private property are, moreover, identical expressions: in the one the same thing is affirmed with reference to activity as is affirmed in the other with reference to the product of the activity.

Further, the division of labour implies the contradiction between the interest of the separate individual or the individual family and the communal interest of all individuals who have intercourse with one another. And indeed, this communal interest does not exist merely in the imagination, as "the general good," but first of all in reality, as the mutual interdependence of the individuals among whom the labour is divided. And finally, the division of labour offers us the first example of how, as long as man remains in natural society,[19] that is as long as a cleavage exists between the particular and the common interest, as long therefore as activity is not voluntarily, but naturally, divided, man's own deed becomes an alien power opposed to him, which enslaves him instead of being controlled by him. For as soon as labour is distributed, each man has a particular, exclusive sphere of activity, which is forced upon him and from which he cannot escape. He is a hunter, a fisherman, a shepherd, or a critical critic, and must remain so if he does not want to lose his means of livelihood; while in communist society, where nobody has one exclusive sphere of activity but each can become accomplished in any branch he wishes, society regulates the general production and thus makes it possible for me to do one thing to-day and another to-morrow, to hunt in the morning, fish in the afternoon, rear cattle in the evening, criticize after dinner, just as I have a mind, without ever becoming hunter, fisherman, shepherd or critic.

This crystallization of social activity, this consolidation of what we ourselves produce into an objective

power above us, growing out of our control, thwarting
our expectations, bringing to naught our calculations, is
one of the chief factors in historical development up
till now. And out of this very contradiction between
the interest of the individual and that of the community the latter takes an independent form as the
STATE, divorced from the real interests of individual and
community, and at the same time as an illusory communal
life, always based, however, on the real ties existing in
every family and tribal conglomeration (such as flesh
and blood, language, division of labour on a larger
scale, and other interests) and especially, as we shall
enlarge upon later, on the classes, already determined
by the division of labour, which in every such mass of
men separate out, and of which one dominates all the
others. It follows from this that all struggles within
the State, the struggle between democracy, aristocracy
and monarchy, the struggle for the franchise, etc., etc.,
are merely the illusory forms in which the real struggles
of the different classes are fought out among one another
(of this the German theoreticians have not the faintest
inkling, although they have received a sufficient introduction to the subject in *The German-French Annals*[20]
and *The Holy Family*[21]).

Further, it follows that every class which is struggling
for mastery, even when its domination, as is the case
with the proletariat, postulates the abolition of the
old form of society in its entirety and of mastery itself,
must first conquer for itself political power in order to
represent its interest in turn as the general interest,
a step to which in the first moment it is forced. Just
because individuals seek *only* their particular interest,
i.e. that not coinciding with their communal interest
(for the "general good" is the illusory form of communal life), the latter will be imposed on them as an
interest "alien" to them, and "independent" of them,

as in its turn a particular, peculiar "general interest"; or they must meet face to face in this antagonism, as in democracy.²² On the other hand too, the *practical* struggle of these particular interests, which constantly *really* run counter to the communal and illusory communal interests, make *practical* intervention and control necessary through the illusory "general-interest" in the form of the State. The social power, i.e. the multiplied productive force, which arises through the co-operation of different individuals as it is determined within the division of labour, appears to these individuals, since their co-operation is not voluntary but natural, not as their own united power but as an alien force existing outside them, of the origin and end of which they are ignorant, which they thus cannot control, which on the contrary passes through a peculiar series of phases and stages independent of the will and the action of man, nay even being the prime governor of these.

This "estrangement"²³ (to use a term which will be comprehensible to the philosophers) can, of course, only be abolished given two *practical* premises. For it to become an "intolerable" power, i.e. a power against which men make a revolution, it must necessarily have rendered the great mass of humanity "propertyless," and produced, at the same time, the contradiction of an existing world of wealth and culture, both of which conditions presuppose a great increase in productive power, a high degree of its development. And, on the other hand, this development of productive forces (which itself implies the actual empirical existence of men in their *world-historical*, instead of local, being) is absolutely necessary as a practical premise: firstly, for the reason that without it only *want* is made general, and with want the struggle for necessities and all the old filthy business would necessarily be reproduced; and secondly, because only with this universal development of productive forces is a *universal* intercourse between men established, which produces in all nations simultaneously the phenomenon of the "propertyless" mass (universal competition), makes each nation dependent on the revolutions of the others, and finally has put *world-historical*, empirically universal individuals in place of local ones. Without this, (1) Communism could only exist as a local event; (2) The forces of intercourse themselves could not have developed as universal, hence intolerable powers: they would have remained homebred superstitious conditions; and (3) Each extension of intercourse would abolish local communism. Empirically, communism is only possible as the act of the dominant peoples "all at once" or simultaneously, which presupposes the universal development of productive forces and the world-intercourse bound up with them. How otherwise could property have had a history at all, have taken on different forms, and landed property, for instance, according to the different premises given, have proceeded in France from parcellation to centralization in the hands of a few, in England from centralization in the hands of a few to parcellation, as is actually the case to-day?[24] Or how does it happen that trade, which after all is nothing more than the exchange of products of various individuals and countries, rules the whole world through the relation of supply and demand—a relation which, as an English economist says, hovers over the earth like the Fate of the Ancients, and with invisible hand allots fortune and misfortune to men, sets up empires and overthrows empires, causes nations to rise and to disappear—while with the abolition of the basis of private property, with the communistic regulation of production (and, implicit in this, the destruction of the alien relation between men and what they themselves produce), the power of the relation of supply and demand is dissolved into nothing, and men get exchange, production, the mode of their mutual relation, under their own control again?

Communism is for us not a stable state which is to be established, an *ideal* to which reality will have to adjust itself. We call communism the *real* movement which abolishes the present state of things. The conditions of this movement result from the premises now in existence. Besides, the world-market is presupposed by the mass of propertyless workers—labour-power cut off as a mass from capital or from even a limited satisfaction—and therefore no longer by the mere precariousness of labour, which, not giving an assured livelihood, is often lost through competition. The proletariat can thus only exist *world-historically*, just as communism, its movement, can only have a "world-historical" existence. World-historical existence of individuals, i.e. existence of individuals which is directly linked up with world history.

The form of intercourse determined by the existing productive forces at all previous historical stages, and in its turn determining these, is *civil society*.[25] This, as is clear from what we have said above, has as its premises and basis the simple family and the multiple, the so-called tribe, the more precise determinants of which are enumerated in our remarks above. Already here we see how this civil society is the true source and theatre of all history, and how nonsensical is the conception of history held hitherto, which neglects the real relationships and confines itself to high-sounding dramas of princes and states. Civil society embraces the whole material intercourse of individuals within a definite stage of the development of productive forces. It embraces the whole commercial and industrial life of this stage and, in so far, transcends the State and the nation, though, on the other hand again, it must assert itself towards foreign peoples as nationality, and inwardly must organize itself as State. The word "civil society" emerged in the eighteenth century, when property relationships had already extricated themselves from the ancient and medieval communal society. Civil society as such only develops with the bourgeoisie; the social organization evolving directly out of production and commerce, which in all ages forms the basis of the State and of the rest of the idealistic superstructure, has, however, always been designated by the same name.

*(b) Concerning the Production of Consciousness.*

In history up to the present it is certainly an empirical fact that separate individuals have, with the broadening of their activity into world-historical activity, become more and more enslaved under a power alien to them (a pressure which they have conceived of as a dirty trick on the part of the so-called universal spirit), a power which has become more and more enormous and, in the last instance, turns out to be the *world-market*. But it is just as empirically established that, by the overthrow of the existing state of society by the communist revolution (of which more below) and the abolition of private property which is identical with it, this power, which so baffles the German theoreticians, will be dissolved; and that then the liberation of each single individual will be accomplished in the measure in which history becomes transformed into world-history. From the above it is clear that the real intellectual wealth of the individual depends entirely on the wealth of his real connections. Only then will the separate individuals be liberated from the various national and local barriers, be brought into practical connection with the material and intellectual production of the whole world and be put in a position to acquire the capacity to enjoy this all-sided production of the whole earth (the creations of man). Universal dependence, this natural form of the world-historical co-operation of individuals, will be transformed by this communist revolution into the control and conscious mastery of these powers, which, born of the action of men on one another, have till now overawed and governed men as powers completely alien to them. Now this view can be expressed again in speculative-idealistic, i.e. fantastic, terms as " spontaneous generation of the species," ("society as the subject"), and thereby the series of inter-related individuals can be conceived as a single individual, which accomplishes the mystery of generating itself. It is clear here that individuals certainly make one another, physically and mentally, but do not make themselves either in the non-sense of Saint Bruno, nor in the sense of the "unique," of the "made" man.[26]

Our conception of history depends on our ability to expound the real process of production, starting out from the simple material production of life, and to comprehend the form of intercourse connected with this and created by this (i.e. civil society in its various stages), as the basis of all history; further, to show it in its action as State; and so, from this starting-point, to explain the whole mass of different theoretical products and forms of consciousness, religion, philosophy, ethics etc., etc., and trace their origins and growth, by which means, of course, the whole thing can be shown in its totality (and therefore, too, the reciprocal action of these various sides on one another). It has not, like the idealistic view of history, in every period to look for a category, but remains constantly on the real ground of history; it does not explain practice from the idea but explains the formation of ideas from material practice; and accordingly it comes to the conclusion that all forms and products of consciousness cannot be dissolved by mental criticism, by resolution into " self-consciousness " or transformation into " apparitions," " spectres," " fancies," etc., but only by the practical overthrow of the actual social relations which gave rise to this idealistic humbug; that not criticism but revolution is the driving force of history, also of religion, of philosophy and all other types of theory. It shows that history does not end by being resolved into "self-consciousness" as "spirit of the spirit," but that in it at each stage there is found a material result: a sum of productive forces, a historically created relation of individuals to nature and to one another, which is handed down to each generation from its predecessor; a mass of productive forces, different forms of capital, and conditions, which, indeed, is modified by the new generation on the one hand, but also on the other prescribes for it its conditions of life and gives it a definite development, a special character. It shows that circumstances make men just as much as men make circumstances.

This sum of productive forces, forms of capital and social forms of intercourse, which every individual and generation finds in existence as something given, is the real basis of what the philosophers have conceived as "substance" and "essence of man", and what they have deified and attacked: a real basis which is not in the least disturbed, in its effect and influence on the development of men, by the fact that these philosophers revolt against it as "self-consciousness" and "the unique." These conditions of life, which different generations find in existence, decide also whether or not the periodically recurring revolutionary convulsion will be strong enough to overthrow the basis of all existing forms. And if these material elements of a complete revolution are not present (namely, on the one hand the existence of productive forces, on the other the formation of a revolutionary mass, which revolts not only against separate conditions of society up till then, but against the very "production of life" till then, the "total activity" on which it was based), then, as far as practical development is concerned, it is absolutely immaterial whether the " idea " of this revolution has been expressed a hundred times already; as the history of communism proves.

In the whole conception of history up to the present this real basis of history has either been totally neglected or else considered as a minor matter quite irrelevant to the course of history. History must therefore always be written according to an extraneous standard ; the real production of life seems to be beyond history, while the truly historical appears to be separated from ordinary life, something extra-superterrestrial. With this the relation of man to nature is excluded from history and hence the antithesis of nature and history is created. The exponents of this conception of history have consequently only been able to see in history the political actions of princes and States, religious and all sorts of theoretical struggles, and in particular in each historical epoch have had to share the *illusion of that epoch*. For instance, if an epoch imagines itself to be actuated by purely " political " or " religious " motives, although " religion " and " politics " are only forms of its true motives, the historian accepts this opinion. The " idea," the " conception " of these conditioned men about their real practice, is transformed into the sole determining, active force, which controls and determines their practice. When the crude form in which the division of labour appears with the Indians and Egyptians calls forth the caste-system in their State and religion, the historian believes that the caste-system is the power which has produced this crude social form. While the French and the English at least hold by the political illusion, which is moderately close to reality, the Germans move in the realm of the "pure spirit", and make religious illusion the driving force of history.

The Hegelian philosophy of history is the last consequence, reduced to its "finest expression," of all this German historiography, for which it is not a question of real, nor even of political, interests, but of pure thoughts, which inevitably appear, even to Saint Bruno, as a series of "thoughts" that devour one another and are finally swallowed up in "self-consciousness." And equally inevitably, and more logically, the course of history appears to the Blessed Max Stirner, who knows not a thing about real history, as a mere tale of "knights," robbers and ghosts, from whose visions he can, of course, only save himself by "unholiness." This conception is truly religious: it postulates religious man as the primitive man, and in its imagination puts the religious production of fancies in the place of the real production of the means of subsistence and of life itself. This whole conception of history, together with its dissolution and the scruples and qualms resulting from it, is a purely *national* affair of the Germans and has only *local* interest for the Germans, as for instance the important question treated several times of late: how really we " pass from the realm of God to the realm of man "—as if this " realm of God " had ever existed anywhere save in the imagination, and the learned gentlemen, without being aware of it, were not constantly living in the " realm of man " to which they are now seeking the way; and as if the learned pastime (for it is nothing more) of explaining the mystery of this theoretical bubble-blowing did not on the contrary lie in demonstrating its origin in actual earthly conditions.

Always, for these Germans, it is simply a matter of resolving the nonsense of earlier writers into some other freak, i.e. of presupposing that all this nonsense has a special meaning which can be discovered; while really it is only a question of explaining this theoretical talk from the actual existing conditions. The real, practical dissolution of these phrases, the removal of these notions from the consciousness of men, will, as we have already said, be effected by altered circumstances, not by theoretical deductions. For the mass of men, i.e. the proletariat, these theoretical notions do not exist and hence do not require to be dissolved, and if this mass ever had any theoretical notions, e.g. religion, etc., these have now long been dissolved by circumstances. The purely national character of these questions and solutions is shown again in the way these theorists believe in all seriousness that chimeras like "the God-Man," "Man," etc., have presided over individual epochs of history (Saint Bruno even goes so far as to assert that " only criticism and critics have made history ") and when they themselves construct historical systems, they skip over all earlier periods in the greatest haste and pass immediately from Mongolism to history " with meaningful content," that is to say, to the history of the Halle and German Annals[27] and the dissolution of the Young-Hegelian school into a general squabble. They forget all other nations, all real events, and the *theatrum mundi*[28] is confined to the Leipzig Book Fair and the mutual quarrels of " Criticism," " Man," and " the Unique."

If these theorists treat really historical subjects, as for instance the eighteenth century, they merely give a history of the ideas of the times, torn away from the facts and the practical development fundamental to them ; and even then they only give these ideas in order to represent them as an imperfect preliminary stage, the as yet limited predecessor of the real historical age, i.e. the period of the German philosophic struggle from 1840 to 1844. As might be expected when the history of an earlier period is written with the aim of accentuating the brilliance of an unhistoric person and his fantasies, all the really historic events, even the really historic invasions of politics into history, receive no mention.

Instead we get a narrative based on systematic constructions and literary gossip, such as Saint Bruno provided in his now forgotten history of the eighteenth century.[29] These high-falutin, bombastic hucksters of ideas, who imagine themselves infinitely exalted above all national prejudices, are thus in practice far more national than the beer-quaffing German philistines who dream of a united Germany. They do not recognize the deeds of other nations as historical: they live in Germany, to Germany, and for Germany; they turn the Rhine-song into a religious hymn and conquer Alsace-Lorraine by robbing French philosophy instead of the French State, by Germanizing French ideas instead of French provinces. Herr Venedey is a cosmopolitan compared with the Saints Bruno and Max, who, in the universal dominance of theory, proclaim the universal dominance of Germany.

It is also clear from these arguments how grossly Feuerbach is deceiving himself, when (*Wigand's Quarterly* 1845, Vol. 2) by virtue of the qualification "common man" he declares himself a communist, transforms the latter into a predicate of "*man*," and thereby thinks it possible to change the word "communist," which in the real world means the follower of a definite revolutionary party, into a mere category. Feuerbach's whole deduction with regard to the relation of men to one another goes only so far as to prove that men need and always have needed each other. He wants to establish consciousness of this fact, that is to say, like the other theorists, merely to produce a correct consciousness about an existing fact; whereas for the real communist it is a question of overthrowing the existing state of things. We thoroughly appreciate, moreover, that Feuerbach, in endeavouring to produce consciousness of just *this* fact, is going as far as a theorist possibly can, without ceasing to be a theorist and philosopher. It is characteristic, however, that Saint Bruno and Saint Max seize on Feuerbach's conception of the communist and put it in place of the real communist—which occurs, partly, merely in order that they can combat communism too as "spirit of the spirit," as a philosophical category, as an equal opponent and, in the case of Saint Bruno, partly also for pragmatic reasons.

Like our opponents, Feuerbach still accepts and at the same time misunderstands existing reality. We recall the passage in the *Philosophy of the Future*,[30] where he develops the view that the existence of a thing or a man is at the same time its or his essence, that the conditions of existence, the mode of life and particular activity of an animal or human individual are those, in which its " essence " feels itself satisfied. Here every exception is expressly conceived as an unhappy chance, as an abnormality which cannot be altered. Thus if millions of proletarians feel themselves by no means contented in their conditions of life, if their existence [is in contradiction with their " essence," then it is certainly an abnormality, but not an unhappy chance ; an historical fact based on quite definite social relationships. Feuerbach is content to affirm this fact ; he only interprets the existing sensuous world, has only the relation of a theorist to it],[31] while in reality for the practical materialist, i.e. the communist, it is a question of revolutionizing the existing world, of practically attacking and changing existing things. When occasionally we find such views with Feuerbach, they are never more than isolated surmises and have much too little influence on his general outlook to be considered here as anything else than embryos capable of development.

Feuerbach's "interpretation" of the sensuous world is confined on the one hand to mere contemplation of it, and on the other to mere feeling ; he says "man" instead of "real, historical men." "Man" is really "the German." In the first case, the contemplation of the sensuous world, he necessarily lights on things which contradict his consciousness and feeling, which upset the harmony of all parts of the sensuous world and especially of man and nature, a harmony he presupposes.* To push these on one side, he must take refuge in a double perception, a profane one which only perceives the "flatly obvious" and a higher more philosophical one which perceives the "true essence" of things. He does not see how the sensuous world around him is, not a thing given direct from all eternity, ever the same, but the product of industry and of the state of society; and, indeed, in the sense that it is an historical product, the result of the activity of a whole succession of generations, each standing on the shoulders of the preceding one, developing its industry and its intercourse, modifying its social organization according to the changed needs. Even the objects of the simplest "sensuous certainty" are only given him through social development, industry and commercial intercourse. The cherry-tree, like almost all fruit-trees, was, as is well known, only a few centuries ago transplanted by commerce into our zone, and therefore only by this action of a definite society in a definite age provided for the evidence of Feuerbach's "senses." Actually, when we conceive things thus, as they really are and happened, every profound philosophical problem is resolved, as will be seen even more clearly later, quite simply into an empirical fact.

For instance, the important question of the relation of man to nature (Bruno goes so far as to speak of "the antitheses in nature and history", as though these were two separate "things" and man did not

* Feuerbach's failing is not that he subordinates the flatly obvious, the sensuous appearance, to the sensuous reality established by more accurate investigation of the sensuous facts, but that he cannot in the last resort cope with the sensuous world except by looking at it with the "eyes" i.e. through the "spectacles" of the *philosopher*.

always have before him an historical nature and a natural history) out of which all the " unfathomably lofty works " on " substance " and " self-consciousness " were born, crumbles of itself when we understand that the celebrated " unity of man with nature " has always existed in industry and has existed in varying forms in every epoch according to the lesser or greater development of industry, just like the " struggle " of man with nature, right up to the development of his productive powers on a corresponding basis. Industry and commerce, production and the exchange of the necessities of life, themselves determine distribution, the structure of the different social classes and are, in turn, determined by these as to the mode in which they are carried on ; and so it happens that in Manchester, for instance, Feuerbach sees only factories and machines where a hundred years ago only spinning-wheels and weaving-looms were to be seen, or in the Campagna of Rome he finds only pasture lands and swamps, where in the time of Augustus he would have found nothing but the vineyards and villas of Roman capitalists. Feuerbach speaks in particular of the perception of natural science ; he mentions secrets which are disclosed only to the eye of the physicist and chemist : but where would natural science be without industry and commerce ? Even this "pure" natural science is provided with an aim, as with its material, only through trade and industry, through the sensuous activity of men. So much is this activity, this unceasing sensuous labour and creation, this production, the basis of the whole sensuous world as it now exists, that, were it interrupted only for a year, Feuerbach would not only find an enormous change in the natural world, but would very soon find that the whole world of men and his own perceptive faculty, nay his own existence, were missing.

Of course, in all this the priority of external nature

remains unassailed, and all this has no application to the original men produced by "generatio æquivoca" (spontaneous generation) ; but this differentiation has meaning only in so far as man is considered to be distinct from nature. For that matter, nature, the nature that preceded human history, is not by any means the nature in which Feuerbach lives, nor the nature which to-day no longer exists anywhere (except perhaps on a few Australian coral-islands of recent origin) and which, therefore, does not exist for Feuerbach. . . .

Certainly Feuerbach has a great advantage over the "pure" materialists in that he realizes how man too is an "object of the senses." But apart from the fact that he only conceives him as a "sensuous object," not as "sensuous activity," because he still remains in the realm of theory and conceives of men not in their given social connection, not under their existing conditions of life, which have made them what they are, he never arrives at the really existing active men, but stops at the abstraction "man", and gets no further than recognizing "the true, individual, corporeal man" emotionally, i.e. he knows no other "human relationships" "of man to man" than love and friendship, and even then idealized. He gives no criticism of the present conditions of life. Thus he never manages to conceive the sensuous world as the total living sensuous activity of the individuals composing it ; and therefore when, for example, he sees instead of healthy men a crowd of scrofulous, over-worked and consumptive starvelings, he is compelled to take refuge in the "higher perception" and in the ideal "compensation in the species," and thus to relapse into idealism at the very point where the communist materialist sees the necessity, and at the same time the condition, of a transformation both of industry and of the social structure.

As far as Feuerbach is a materialist he does not deal

with history, and as far as he considers history he is not a materialist. With him materialism and history diverge completely, a fact which explains itself from what has been said.³²

History is nothing but the succession of the separate generations, each of which exploits the materials, the forms of capital, the productive forces handed down to it by all preceding ones, and thus on the one hand continues the traditional activity in completely changed circumstances and, on the other, modifies the old circumstances with a completely changed activity. This can be speculatively distorted so that later history is made the goal of earlier history, e.g. the goal ascribed to the discovery of America is to further the eruption of the French Revolution. Thereby history receives its own special aims and becomes " a person ranking with other persons " (to wit : " self-consciousness, criticism, the Unique," etc.), while what is designated with the words " destiny," " goal," " germ," or " idea " of earlier history is nothing more than an abstraction formed from later history, from the active influence which earlier history exercises on later history. The further the separate spheres, which interact on one another, extend in the course of this development, the more the original isolation of the separate nationalities is destroyed by the developed mode of production and intercourse and the division of labour naturally brought forth by these, the more history becomes world-history. Thus, for instance, if in England a machine is invented, which in India or China deprives countless workers of bread, and overturns the whole form of existence of these empires, this invention becomes a world-historical fact. Or again, take the case of sugar and coffee which have proved their world-historical importance in the nineteenth century by the fact that the lack of these products, occasioned by the Napoleonic Continental system, caused the Germans to rise against Napoleon, and thus became the real basis of the glorious Wars of Liberation of 1813. From this it follows that this transformation of history into world-history is not indeed a mere abstract act on the part of the " self-consciousness," the world-spirit, or of any other metaphysical spectre, but a quite material, empirically verifiable act, an act the proof of which every individual furnishes as he comes and goes, eats, drinks and clothes himself.

The ideas of the ruling class are in every epoch the ruling ideas : i.e. the class, which is the ruling material force of society, is at the same time its ruling intellectual force. The class which has the means of material production at its disposal, has control at the same time over the means of mental production, so that thereby, generally speaking, the ideas of those who lack the means of mental production are subject to it. The ruling ideas are nothing more than the ideal expression of the dominant material relationships, the dominant material relationships grasped as ideas ; hence of the relationships which make the one class the ruling one, therefore the ideas of its dominance. The individuals composing the ruling class possess among other things consciousness, and therefore think. In so far, therefore, as they rule as a class and determine the extent and compass of an epoch, it is self-evident that they do this in their whole range, hence among other things rule also as thinkers, as producers of ideas, and regulate the production and distribution of the ideas of their age : thus their ideas are the ruling ideas of the epoch. For instance, in an age and in a country where royal power, aristocracy and bourgeoisie are contending for mastery and where, therefore, mastery is shared, the doctrine of the separation of powers proves to be the dominant idea and is expressed as an " eternal law." The division of labour, which we saw above as one of the chief forces of history up till now, manifests itself also in the ruling class as the division of mental and material labour, so that inside this class one part appears as the thinkers of the class (its active, conceptive ideologists, who make the perfecting of the illusion of the class about itself their chief source of livelihood), while the others' attitude to these ideas and illusions is more passive and receptive, because they are in reality the active members of this class and have less time to make up illusions and ideas about themselves. Within this class this cleavage can even develop into a certain opposition and hostility between the two parts, which, however, in the case of a practical collision, in which the class itself is endangered, automatically comes to nothing, in which case there also vanishes the semblance that the ruling ideas were not the ideas of the ruling class and had a power distinct from the power of this class. The existence of revolutionary ideas in a particular period presupposes the existence of a revolutionary class; about the premises for the latter sufficient has already been said above.

If now in considering the course of history we detach the ideas of the ruling class from the ruling class itself and attribute to them an independent existence, if we confine ourselves to saying that these or those ideas were dominant, without bothering ourselves about the conditions of production and the producers of these ideas, if we then ignore the individuals and world conditions which are the source of the ideas, we can say, for instance, that during the time that the aristocracy was dominant, the concepts honour, loyalty, etc., were dominant, during the dominance of the bourgeoisie the concepts freedom, equality, etc. The ruling class itself on the whole imagines this to be so. This conception of history, which is common to all historians, particularly since the eighteenth century, will necessarily come up against the phenomenon that increasingly abstract ideas hold sway, i.e. ideas which increasingly take on the form of universality. For each new class which puts itself in the place of one ruling before it, is compelled, merely in order to carry through its aim, to represent its interest as the common interest of all the members of society, put in an ideal form; it will give its ideas the form of universality, and represent them as the only rational, universally valid ones. The class making a revolution appears from the very start, merely because it is opposed to a *class*, not as a class but as the representative of the whole of society; it appears as the whole mass of society confronting the one ruling class. It can do this because, to start with, its interest really is more connected with the common interest of all other non-ruling classes, because under the pressure of conditions its interest has not yet been able to develop as the particular interest of a particular class. Its victory, therefore, benefits also many individuals of the other classes which are not winning a dominant position, but only in so far as it now puts these individuals in a position to raise themselves into the ruling class. When the French bourgeoisie overthrew the power of the aristocracy, it thereby made it possible for many proletarians to raise themselves above the proletariat, but only in so far as they became bourgeois. Every new class, therefore, achieves its hegemony only on a broader basis than that of the class ruling previously, in return for which the opposition of the non-ruling class against the new ruling class later develops all the more sharply and profoundly. Both these things determine the fact that the struggle to be waged against this new ruling class, in its turn, aims at a more decided and radical negation of the previous conditions of society than could all previous classes which sought to rule.

This whole semblance, that the rule of a certain class is only the rule of certain ideas, comes to a natural end, of course, as soon as society ceases at last to be organized in the form of class-rule, that is to say as soon as it is no longer necessary to represent a particular interest as general or "the general interest" as ruling.

Once the ruling ideas have been separated from the ruling individuals and, above all, from the relationships which result from a given stage of the mode of production, and in this way the conclusion has been reached that history is always under the sway of ideas, it is very easy to abstract from these various ideas " the idea," " die Idee," etc., as the dominant force in history, and thus to understand all these separate ideas and concepts as " forms of self-determination " on the part of *the* concept developing in history. It follows then naturally, too, that all the relationships of men can be derived from the concept of man, man as conceived, the essence of man, *man*. This has been done by the speculative philosophers. Hegel himself confesses at the end of *Teh Philosophy of History* that he " has considered the progress of *the concept* only " and has represented in history " the true theodicy."³³ Now one can go back again to the " producers of the concept," to the theoreticians, ideologists and philosophers, and one comes then to the conclusion that the philosophers, the thinkers as such, have at all times been dominant in history: a conclusion, as we see, already expressed by Hegel. The whole trick of proving the hegemony of the spirit in history (hierarchy Stirner calls it) is thus confined to the following three tricks.

1. One must separate the ideas of those ruling for empirical reasons, under empirical conditions and as empirical individuals, from these actual rulers, and thus recognize the rule of ideas or illusions in history.

2. One must bring an order into this rule of ideas, prove a mystical connection among the successive ruling ideas, which is managed by understanding them as "acts of self-determination on the part of the concept " (this is possible because by virtue of their empirical basis these ideas are really connected with one another and because, conceived as *mere* ideas, they become self-distinctions, distinctions made by thought).

3. To remove the mystical appearance of this "self-determining concept" it is changed into a person—"self-consciousness"—or, to appear thoroughly materialistic, into a series of persons, who represent the "concept" in history, into the "thinkers," the "philosophers," the ideologists, who again are understood as the manufacturers of history, as "the council of guardians," as the rulers. Thus the whole body of materialistic elements has been removed from history and now full rein can be given to the speculative steed.

Whilst in ordinary life every shopkeeper is very well able to distinguish between what somebody professes to be and what he really is, our historians have not yet won even this trivial insight. They take every epoch at its word and believe that everything it says and imagines about itself is true.

This historical method which reigned in Germany, (and especially the reason why), must be understood from its connection with the illusion of ideologists in general, e.g. the illusions of the jurists, politicians (of the practical statesmen among them, too), from the dogmatic dreamings and distortions of these fellows; this illusion is explained perfectly easily from their practical position in life, their job, and the division of labour.

## 2. THE REAL BASIS OF IDEOLOGY.

### (a) *Intercourse and Productive Power.*

The greatest division of material and mental labour is the separation of town and country. The antagonism between town and country begins with the transition from barbarism to civilization, from tribe to State, from locality to nation, and runs through the whole history of civilization to the present day (the Anti-Corn Law League). The existence of the town implies, at the same time, the necessity of administration, police, taxes, etc., in short, of the municipality, and thus of politics in general. Here first became manifest the division of the population into two great classes, which is directly based on the division of labour and on the instruments of production. The town already is in actual fact the concentration of the population, of the instruments of production, of capital, of pleasures, of needs, while the country demonstrates just the opposite fact, their isolation and separation. The antagonism of town and country can only exist as a result of private property. It is the most crass expression of the subjection of the individual under the division of labour, under a definite activity forced upon him—a subjection which makes one man into a restricted town-animal, the other into a restricted country-animal, and daily creates anew the conflict between their interests. Labour is here again the chief thing, power *over* individuals, and as long as the latter exists, private property must exist. The abolition of the antagonism between town and country is one of the first conditions of communal life, a condition which again depends on a mass of material premises and which cannot be fulfilled by the mere will, as anyone can see at the first glance. (These conditions have still to be enumerated.) The separation of town and country can also be understood as the separation of capital and landed property, as the beginning of the existence and development of capital independent of landed property—the beginning of property having its basis only in labour and exchange.

In the towns which, in the Middle Ages, did not derive ready-made from an earlier period but were formed anew by the serfs who had become free, each man's own particular labour was his only property apart from the small capital he brought with him, consisting almost solely of the most necessary tools of his craft. The competition of serfs constantly escaping into the town, the constant war of the country against the town and thus the necessity of an organized municipal military force, the bond of common ownership in a particular piece of work, the necessity of common buildings for the sale of their wares at a time when craftsmen were at the same time traders, and the consequent exclusion of the unauthorized from these buildings, the conflict among the interests of the various crafts, the necessity of protecting their laboriously acquired skill, and the feudal organization of the whole of the country: these were the causes of the union of the workers of each craft in guilds. We have not at this point to go further into the manifold modifications of the guild system, which arise through later historical developments.

The flight of the serfs into the towns went on without interruption right through the Middle Ages. These serfs, persecuted by their lords in the country, came separately into the towns, where they found an organized community, against which they were powerless, in which they had to subject themselves to the station assigned to them by the demand for their labour and the interest of their organized urban competitors. These workers, entering separately, were never able to attain to any power, since if their labour was of the guild type which had to be learned, the guild-masters bent them to their will and organized them according to their interest; or if their labour was not such as had to be learned, and therefore not of the guild type, they became day-labourers and never managed to organize, remaining an unorganized rabble. The need for day-labourers in the towns created the rabble. These towns were true "associations," called forth by the direct need of providing for the protection of property, and multiplying the means of production and defence of the separate members. The rabble of these towns was devoid of any power, composed as it was of individuals strange to one another who had entered separately, and who stood unorganized over against an organized power, armed for war, and jealously watching over them. The journeymen and apprentices were organized in each craft as it best suited the interest of the masters. The filial relationship in which they stood to their masters gave the latter a double power—on the one hand because of their influence on the whole life of the journeymen, and on the other because, for the journeymen who worked with the same master, it was a real bond, which held them together against the journeymen of other masters and separated them from these. And finally, the journeymen were bound to the existing order by their simple interest in becoming masters themselves. While, therefore, the rabble at least carried out revolts against the whole municipal order, revolts which remained completely ineffective because of their powerlessness, the journeymen never got further than small acts of insubordination within separate guilds, such as belong to the very nature of the guild. The great risings of the Middle Ages all radiated from the country, but equally remained totally ineffective because of the isolation and consequent crudity of the peasants.

In the towns, the division of labour between the individual guilds was as yet quite natural,[34] and, in the guilds themselves, not at all developed between the individual workers. Every workman had to be versed in a whole round of tasks, had to be able to make everything that was to be made with his tools. The limited commerce and the scanty communication between the individual towns, the lack of population and the narrow needs did not allow of a higher division of labour, and therefore every man who wished to become a master had to be proficient in the whole of his craft. Thus there is found with medieval craftsmen an interest in their special work and in proficiency in it, which was capable of rising to a narrow artistic sense. For this very reason, however, every medieval craftsman was completely absorbed in his work, to which he had a contented, slavish relationship, and to which he was subjected to a far greater extent than the modern worker, whose work is a matter of indifference to him.

Capital in these towns was a natural capital, consisting of a house, the tools of the craft, and the natural, hereditary customers; and not being realizable, on account of the backwardness of commerce and the lack of circulation, it descended from father to son. Unlike modern capital, which can be assessed in money and which may be indifferently invested in this thing or that, this capital was directly connected with the particular work of the owner, inseparable from it and to this extent "estate" capital.[35]

The next extension of the division of labour was the separation of production and commerce, the formation of a special class of merchants; a separation which, in the towns bequeathed by a former period, had been handed down (among other things with the Jews) and which very soon appeared in the newly formed ones. With this there was given the possibility of commercial communications transcending the immediate neighbourhood, a possibility, the realization of which depended on the existing means of communication, the state of public safety in the countryside, which was determined by political conditions (during the whole of the Middle Ages, as is well known, the merchants travelled in armed caravans), and on the cruder or more advanced needs (determined by the stage of culture attained) of the region accessible to intercourse. With commerce the prerogative of a particular class, with the extension of trade through the merchants beyond the immediate surroundings of the town, there immediately appears a reciprocal action between production and commerce. The towns enter into relations *with one another*, new tools are brought from one town into the other, and the separation between production and commerce soon calls forth a new division of production between the individual towns, each of which is soon exploiting a predominant branch of industry. The local restrictions of earlier times begin gradually to be broken down.

In the Middle Ages the citizens in each town were compelled to unite against the landed nobility to save their skins. The extension of trade, the establishment of communications, led the separate towns to get to know other towns, which had asserted the same interests in the struggle with the same antagonist. Out of the many local corporations of burghers there arose only gradually the burgher *class*. The conditions of life of the individual burghers became, on account of their antagonism to the existing relationships and of the mode of labour determined by these, conditions which were common to them all and independent of each individual. The burghers had created the conditions in so far as they had torn themselves free from feudal ties, and were created by them in so far as they were determined by their antagonism to the feudal system which they found in existence. When the individual towns began to enter into associations, these common conditions developed into class conditions. The same conditions, the same antagonism, the same interests necessarily called forth on the whole similar customs everywhere. The bourgeoisie itself, with its conditions, develops only gradually, splits according to the division of labour into various fractions and finally absorbs all earlier possessing classes (while it develops the majority of the earlier non-possessing, and a part of the earlier possessing, class into a new class, the proletariat) in the measure to which all earlier property is transformed into industrial or commercial capital. The separate individuals form a class only in so far as they have to

## FEUERBACH

carry on a common battle against another class; otherwise they are on hostile terms with each other as competitors. On the other hand, the class in its turn achieves an independent existence over against the individuals, so that the latter find their conditions of existence predestined, and hence have their position in life and their personal development assigned to them by their class, become subsumed under it. This is the same phenomenon as the subjection of the separate individuals to the division of labour and can only be removed by the abolition of private property and of labour itself. We have already indicated several times how this subsuming of individuals under the class brings with it their subjection to all kinds of ideas, etc.

It depends purely on the extension of commerce whether the productive forces achieved in a locality, especially inventions, are lost for later development or not. As long as there exists no commerce transcending the immediate neighbourhood, every invention must be made separately in each locality, and mere chances such as irruptions of barbaric peoples, even ordinary wars, are sufficient to cause a country with advanced productive forces and needs to have to start right over again from the beginning. In primitive history every invention had to be made daily anew and in each locality independently. How little highly developed productive forces are safe from complete destruction, given even a relatively very extensive commerce, is proved by the Phœnicians, whose inventions were for the most part lost for a long time to come through the ousting of this nation from commerce, its conquest by Alexander and its consequent decline. Likewise, for instance, glass-painting in the Middle Ages. Only when commerce has become world-commerce and has as its basis big industry, when all nations are drawn into the competitive struggle, is the permanence of the acquired productive forces assured.

The immediate consequence of the division of labour between the various towns was the rise of manufactures, branches of production which had outgrown the guild-system. Manufactures first flourished, in Italy and later in Flanders, under the historical premise of commerce with foreign nations. In other countries, England and France for example, manufactures were at first confined to the home market. Besides the premises already mentioned manufactures depend on yet another: an already advanced concentration of population, particularly in the countryside, and of capital, which began to accumulate in the hands of individuals, partly in the guilds in spite of the guild regulations, partly among the merchants.

That labour which from the first presupposed a machine, even of the crudest sort, soon showed itself the most capable of development. Weaving, earlier carried on in the country by the peasants as a secondary occupation to procure their clothing, was the first labour to receive an impetus and a further development through the extension of commerce. Weaving was the first and remained the principal manufacture. The rising demand for clothing materials, consequent on the growth of population, the growing accumulation and mobilization[36] of natural capital through accelerated circulation, the demand for luxuries called forth by the latter and favoured generally by the gradual extension of commerce, gave weaving a quantitative and qualitative stimulus, which wrenched it out of the form of production hitherto existing. Alongside the peasants weaving for their own use, who continued with this sort of work, there emerged a new class of weavers in the towns, whose fabrics were destined for the whole home market and usually for foreign markets too. Weaving, an occupation demanding in most cases little skill and soon splitting up into countless branches, by its whole nature resisted the trammels of the guild. Weaving was therefore carried on mostly in villages and market-centres without guild organization, which gradually became towns, and indeed the most flourishing towns in each land. With guild-free manufacture, property relations also quickly changed. The first advance beyond natural, estate-capital[37] was provided by the rise of merchants whose capital was from the beginning movable,[38] capital in the modern sense as far as one can speak of it, given the circumstances of those times. The second advance came with manufacture, which again made mobile a mass of natural capital, and altogether increased the mass of movable capital as against that of natural capital. At the same time, manufacture became a refuge of the peasants from the guilds which excluded them or paid them badly, just as earlier the guild-towns had served as a refuge for the peasants from the oppressive landed nobility.

Simultaneously with the beginning of manufactures there was a period of vagabondage caused by the decline of the feudal bodies of retainers, the disbanding of the swollen armies which had flocked to serve the kings against their vassals, the improvement of agriculture, and the transformation of great strips of tillage into pasture-land. From this alone it is clear how this vagabondage is strictly connected with the disintegration of the feudal system. As early as the thirteenth century we find isolated epochs of this kind, but only at the end of the fifteenth and beginning of the sixteenth does this vagabondage make a general and permanent appearance. These vagabonds, who were so numerous that Henry VIII of England had 72,000 of them hanged, were only prevailed upon to work with the greatest difficulty and through the most extreme necessity, and then only after long resistance. The rapid rise of manufactures, particularly in England, absorbed them gradually. With the advent of manufactures, the various nations entered into a competitive relationship, the struggle for trade, which was fought out in wars, protective duties and prohibitions, whereas earlier the nations, in so far as they were connected at all, had carried on an inoffensive exchange with each other. Trade had from now on a political significance.

With manufacture was given simultaneously a changed relationship between worker and employer. In the guilds the patriarchal relationship between journeyman and master maintained itself; in manufacture its place was taken by the monetary relation between worker and capitalist—a relationship which in the countryside and in small towns retained a patriarchal tinge, but in the larger, the real manufacturing towns, quite early lost almost all patriarchal complexion.

Manufacture and the movement of production in general received an enormous impetus through the extension of commerce which came with the discovery of America and the sea-route to the East Indies. The new products imported thence, particularly the masses of gold and silver which came into circulation and totally changed the position of the classes towards one another, dealing a hard blow to feudal landed property and to the workers; the expeditions of adventurers, colonization; and above all the extension of markets into a world-market, which had now become possible and was daily becoming more and more a fact, called forth a new phase of historical development, into which in general we cannot here enter further. Through the colonization of the newly discovered countries the commercial struggle of the nations amongst one another was given new fuel and accordingly greater extension and animosity.

The expansion of trade and manufacture accelerated the accumulation of movable capital, while in the guilds, which were not stimulated to extend their production, natural capital remained stationary or even declined. Trade and manufacture created the big bourgeoisie: in the guilds was concentrated the petty bourgeoisie, which no longer was dominant in the towns as formerly, but had to bow to the might of the great merchants and manufacturers. Hence the decline of the guilds, as soon as they came into contact with manufacture.

The material, commercial relations of nations took on, in the epoch of which we have been speaking, two different forms. At first the small quantity of gold and silver in circulation involved the ban on the export of these metals; and industry, for the most part imported from abroad and made necessary by the need for employing the growing urban population, could not do without those privileges which could be granted not only, of course, against home competition, but chiefly against foreign. The local guild privilege was in these original prohibitions extended over the whole nation. Customs duties originated from the tributes exacted by the feudal lords from merchants passing through their territories, tributes later imposed likewise by the towns, and which, with the rise of the modern states, were the treasury's most obvious means of raising money. The appearance of American gold and silver on the European markets, the gradual development of industry, the rapid expansion of trade and the consequent rise of the non-guild bourgeoisie and of money, gave these measures another significance. The State, which was daily less and less able to do without money, now retained the ban on the export of gold and silver out of fiscal considerations; the bourgeois, who had as their chief object the cornering of these masses of money which were hurled on to the market, were thoroughly content with this; privileges established earlier became a source of income for the government and were sold for money; in the customs legislation there appeared the export-duty, which, since it only placed a hindrance in the way of industry, had a purely fiscal aim.

The second period began in the middle of the seventeenth century and lasted almost to the end of the eighteenth. Commerce and navigation had expanded more rapidly than manufacture, which played a secondary role; the colonies were becoming considerable consumers; and after long struggles the separate nations shared out the opening world-market among themselves. This period begins with the Navigation Laws and colonial monopolies. The competition of the nations among themselves was excluded as far as possible by tariffs, prohibitions and treaties; and in the last resort the competitive struggle was carried on and decided by wars (especially naval wars). The mightiest maritime nation, the English, retained preponderance in trade and manufacture. Here, already, we find concentration on one country. Manufacture was all the time sheltered by protective duties in the home market, by monopolies in the colonial market, and abroad as much as possible by differential duties. The working-up of home-produced material was encouraged (wool and linen in England, silk in France), the export of home-produced raw material forbidden (wool in England), and that of imported material neglected or suppressed (cotton in England). The nation dominant in sea-trade and colonial power naturally secured for itself also the greatest quantitative and qualitative expansion of manufacture. Manufacture could not be carried on without protection, since, if the slightest change takes place in other countries, it can lose its market and be ruined; under reasonably favourable conditions it may easily be introduced into a country, but for this very reason can easily be destroyed. At the same time through the mode in which it is carried on, particularly in the eighteenth century, in the countryside, it is so interwoven with the vital relationships of a great mass of individuals, that no country dare jeopardize their existence by permitting free competition. In so far as it manages to export, it therefore depends entirely on the extension or restriction of commerce, and exercises a relatively very small reaction on the latter. Hence its secondary importance and the influence of the merchants in the eighteenth century. It was especially the merchants and shippers who more than anybody else pressed for State protection and monopolies; the manufacturers demanded and indeed received protection, but all the time were inferior in political importance to the merchants. The commercial towns, particularly the maritime towns, won to some extent the civilized outlook of the big bourgeoisie, but in the factory towns an extreme petty-bourgeois outlook persisted. Cf. Aikin, etc. The eighteenth century was the century of trade. Pinto says this expressly: "*Le commerce fait la marotte du siècle,*" ("Commerce is the rage of the century"); and, "*depuis quelque temps il n'est plus question que de commerce, de navigation et de marine*" ("for some time now people have been talking only about commerce, navigation, and the navy").*

This period is also characterized by the cessation of the bans on the export of gold and silver and the beginning of the bullion-trade; by banks, national debts, paper-money; by speculation in stocks and shares and stock-

*The movement of capital, although considerably accelerated, still remained, however, relatively slow. The splitting-up of the world-market into separate parts, each of which was exploited by a particular nation, the exclusion of competition among themselves on the part of the nations, the clumsiness of production itself and the fact that finance was only evolving from its early stages, greatly impeded circulation. The consequence of this was a haggling, mean and niggardly spirit which still clung to all merchants and to the whole mode of carrying on trade. Compared with the manufacturers, and above all with the craftsmen, they were certainly big bourgeois; compared with the merchants and industrialists of the next period they remain petty bourgeois, cf. Adam Smith.

jobbing in all articles ; by the development of finance in general. Again capital lost a great part of the natural character which had clung to it.

The concentration of trade and manufacture in one country, England, developing irresistibly in the seventeenth century, gradually created for this country a relative world-market, and thus a demand for the manufactured products of this country, which could no longer be met by the industrial productive forces hitherto existing. This demand, outgrowing the productive forces, was the motive power which, by producing big industry—the application of elemental forces to industrial ends, machinery and the most complex division of labour—called into existence the third period of private ownership since the Middle Ages. There already existed in England the other pre-conditions of this new phase: freedom of competition inside the nation, the development of theoretical mechanics, etc. Indeed, the science of mechanics perfected by Newton was altogether the most popular science in France and England in the eighteenth century. (Free competition inside the nation itself had everywhere to be conquered by a revolution—1640 and 1688 in England, 1789 in France.) Competition soon compelled every country that wished to retain its historical role to protect its manufactures by renewed customs regulations (the old duties were no longer any good against big industry); and soon after to introduce big industry under protective duties.

Big industry universalized competition in spite of these protective measures (it is practical free trade ; the duty is only a palliative, a barrier *within* free trade), established means of communication and the modern world market, subordinated trade to itself, transformed all capital into industrial capital, and thus produced the rapid circulation (the financial system is perfected) and the centralization of the various forms of capital. By universal competition it forced all individuals to strain their energy to the utmost. It destroyed as far as possible ideology, religion, morality, etc., and where it could not do this, made them into a palpable lie. It produced world-history for the first time, in so far as it made all civilized nations and every individual member of them dependent for the satisfaction of their wants on the whole world, thus destroying the former natural exclusiveness of separate nations. It made natural science subservient to capital and took from the division of labour the last semblance of its natural character. It destroyed natural growth in general, as far as this is possible while labour exists, and resolved all natural relationships into money relationships. In the place of natural towns it created the modern, large industrial cities which have sprung up over-night. Wherever it penetrated, it destroyed the crafts and all earlier stages of industry. It completed the victory of the commercial town over the countryside. Its first premise was the automatic system. Its development produced a mass of productive forces, for which private property became just as much a fetter as the guild had been for manufacture and the small, rural workshop for the developing craft. These productive forces received under the system of private property a one-sided development only, and became for the most part destructive forces; moreover, a great multitude of such forces could find no application at all within this system. Generally speaking, it created everywhere the same relations between the classes of society, and thus destroyed the peculiar individuality of the various nationalities. And finally, while the bourgeoisie of each nation still retained separate national interests, big industry created a class, which in all nations has the same interest and with which nationality is already dead; a class which is really rid of all the old world and at the same time stands pitted against it. For the worker it makes not only the relation to the capitalist, but labour itself, unbearable.

It is evident that big industry does not reach the same level of development in all districts of a country. This does not, however, retard the class movement of the proletariat, because the proletarians created by big industry assume leadership of this movement and carry the whole mass along with them, and because the workers excluded from big industry are placed by it in a still worse situation than the workers in big industry themselves. The countries in which big industry is developed act in a similar manner upon the more or less non-industrial countries, in so far as the latter are swept by universal commerce into the universal competitive struggle.* These different forms are just so many forms of the organization of labour, and hence of property. In each period a unification of the existing productive forces takes place, in so far as this has been rendered necessary by needs.

(b) *The Relation of State and Law*[39] *to Property.*

The first form of property, in the ancient world as in the Middle Ages, is tribal property, determined with the Romans chiefly by war, with the Germans by the rearing of cattle. In the case of the ancient peoples, since several tribes live together in one town, the tribal property appears as State property, and the right of the individual to it as mere "*possession*" which, however,

---

*Competition makes individuals, not only the bourgeois but still more the workers, mutually hostile, in spite of the fact that it brings them together. Hence it is a long time before these individuals can unite, apart from the fact that for the purposes of this union—if it is not to be merely local—the necessary means, the great industrial cities and cheap and quick communications, have first to be produced by big industry. Hence every organized power standing over against these isolated individuals, who live in relationships daily reproducing this isolation, can only be overcome after long struggles. To demand the opposite would be tantamount to demanding that competition should not exist in this definite epoch of history, or that the individuals should banish from their minds relationships over which in their isolation they have no control.

like tribal property as a whole, is confined to landed property only. Real private property began with the ancients, as with modern nations, with personal movable property—(slavery and community) (*dominium ex jure Quiritium*).[40] In the case of the nations which grew out of the Middle Ages, tribal property evolved through various stages—feudal landed property, corporative movable property, manufacture-capital—to modern capital, determined by big industry and universal competition, i.e. pure private property, which has cast off all semblance of a communal institution and has shut out the State from any influence on the development of property. To this modern private property corresponds the modern State, which, purchased gradually by the owners of property by means of taxation, has fallen entirely into their hands through the national debt, and its existence has become wholly dependent on the commercial credit which the owners of property, the bourgeois, extend to it in the rise and fall of State funds on the stock exchange. By the mere fact that it is a *class* and no longer an *estate*, the bourgeoisie is forced to organize itself no longer locally, but nationally, and to give a general form to its mean average interest. Through the emancipation of private property from the community, the State has become a separate entity, beside and outside civil society; but it is nothing more than the form of organization which the bourgeois necessarily adopt both for internal and external purposes, for the mutual guarantee of their property and interests. The independence of the State is only found nowadays in those countries where the estates have not yet completely developed into classes, where the estates, done away with in more advanced countries, still have a part to play, and where there exists a mixture; countries, that is to say in which no one section of the population can achieve dominance over the others. This is the case particularly in Germany. The most perfect example of the modern State is North America. The modern French, English and American writers all express the opinion that the State exists only for the sake of private property, so that this fact has penetrated into the consciousness of the normal man.

Since the State is the form in which the individuals of a ruling class assert their common interests, and in which the whole civil society of an epoch is epitomized, it follows that in the formation of all communal institutions the State acts as intermediary, that these institutions receive a political form. Hence the illusion that law is based on the will, and indeed on the will divorced from its real basis—on free will. Similarly, the theory of law is in its turn reduced to the actual laws.

Civil law develops simultaneously with private property out of the disintegration of the natural community. With the Romans the development of private property and civil law had no further industrial and commercial consequences, because their whole mode of production did not alter. With modern peoples, where the feudal community was disintegrated by industry and trade, there began with the rise of private property and civil law a new phase, which was capable of further development. The very first town which carried on an extensive trade in the Middle Ages, Amalfi, also developed maritime law. As soon as industry and trade developed private property further, first in Italy and later in other countries, Roman civil law was adopted again in a perfected form and raised to authority. When later the bourgeoisie had acquired so much power that the princes took up their interests in order to overthrow the feudal nobility by means of the bourgeoisie, there began in all countries—in France in the sixteenth century— the real development of law, which in all countries except England proceeded on the basis of the Roman

Codex. In England too, Roman legal principles had to be introduced to further the development of civil law (especially in the case of personal movable property). It must not be forgotten that law has just as little an independent history as religion.

In civil law the existing property relationships are declared to be the result of the general will. The *jus utendi et abutendi*[41] itself asserts on the one hand the fact that private property has become entirely independent of the community, and on the other the illusion that private property itself is based on the private will, the arbitrary disposal of the thing. In practice, the *abuti* has very definite economic limitations for the owner of private property, if he does not wish to see his property and hence his *jus abutendi* pass into other hands, since actually the thing, considered merely with reference to his will, is not a thing at all, but only becomes true property in intercourse, and independently of the right to the thing (a *relationship*, which the philosophers call an idea). This juridical illusion, which reduces law to the mere will, necessarily leads, in the further development of property relationships, to the position that a man may have a title to a thing without really having the thing. If, for instance, the income from a piece of land is lost owing to competition, then the proprietor has certainly his legal title to it along with the *jus utendi et abutendi*. But he can do nothing with it; he owns nothing as a landed proprietor if he has not enough capital besides to cultivate his ground. This illusion of the jurists also explains the fact that for them, as for every codex, it is altogether fortuitous that individuals enter into relationships among themselves (e.g. contracts); it explains why they consider that these relationships can be entered into or not at will, and that their content rests purely on the individual free will of the contracting parties. Whenever, through the development of industry and commerce, new forms of intercourse have been evolved, (e.g. assurance companies etc.) the law has always been compelled to admit them among the modes of acquiring property.

．　．　．　．　．

Nothing is more common than the notion that in history up till now it has only been a question of "*taking*." The barbarians "take" the Roman Empire, and this fact of "taking" is made to explain the transition from the old world to the feudal system. In this taking by barbarians, however, the question is, whether the nation which is conquered has evolved industrial productive forces, as is the case with modern peoples, or whether their productive forces are based for the most part merely on their association and on the community. Taking is further determined by the object taken. A banker's fortune, consisting of paper, cannot be taken at all, without the taker's submitting to the conditions of production and intercourse of the country taken. Similarly the total industrial capital of a modern industrial country. And finally, everywhere there is very soon an end to taking, and when there is nothing more to take, you have to set about producing. From this necessity of producing, which very soon asserts itself, it follows that the form of community adopted by the settling conquerors must correspond to the stage of development of the productive forces they find in existence; or, if this is not the case from the start, it must change according to the productive forces. By this, too, is explained the fact, which people profess to have noticed everywhere in the period following the migration of the peoples, namely that the servant was master, and that the conquerors very soon took over language, culture and manners from the conquered. The feudal system was by no means brought complete from Germany, but had its origin, as far as the conquerors were concerned, in the martial organization of the army during the actual conquest, and this only evolved after the conquest into the feudal system proper through the action of the productive forces found in the conquered countries. To what an extent this form was determined by the productive forces is shown by the abortive attempts to realize other forms derived from reminiscences of ancient Rome (Charlemagne, etc.).

(c) *Natural and Civilized Instruments of Production and Forms of Property.*

(*Gap in manuscript*).... From the first, there follows the premise of a highly developed division of labour and an extensive commerce; from the second, the locality. In the first case the individuals must be brought together, in the second they find themselves alongside the given instrument of production as instruments of production themselves. Here, therefore, arises the difference between natural instruments of production and those created by civilization. The field (water, etc.) can be regarded as a natural instrument of production. In the first case, that of the natural instrument of production, individuals are subservient to nature; in the second, to a product of labour. In the first case, therefore, property (landed property) appears as direct natural domination, in the second as domination of labour, particularly of accumulated labour, capital. The first case presupposes that the individuals are united by some bond, family, tribe, the land itself, etc.; the second that they are independent of one another and are only held together by exchange. In the first case, what is involved is chiefly an exchange between men and nature, in which the labour of the former is exchanged for the products of the latter; in the second, it is predominantly an exchange of men among themselves. In the first case, average, human common-sense is adequate—physical and mental activity are as yet not separated at all; in the second, the division between physical and mental labour must already be practically completed. In the first case, the domination of the proprietor over the propertyless may be based on a personal relationship, on a kind of community; in the second, it must have taken on a material shape in a third party—money. In the first case, small industry exists, but determined by the utilization of the natural instrument of production and therefore without the distribution of labour among various individuals; in the second, industry exists only in and through the division of labour.

Our investigation hitherto started from the instruments of production, and we have seen the necessity of private property for certain industrial stages. In *industrie extractive*[42] private property still coincides with labour; in small industry and all agriculture up till now property is the necessary consequence of the existing instruments of production; in big industry the contradiction between the instrument of production and private property is the product of big industry and only appears with it; moreover, big industry must be highly developed to produce this contradiction. And thus only with big industry does the abolition of private property become possible.

In big industry and competition the whole mass of conditions of existence, limitations, biases of individuals, are fused together into the two simplest forms : private property and labour. With money every form of intercourse, and intercourse itself, is considered fortuitous for the individuals. Thus money implies that all previous intercourse was only intercourse of individuals under particular conditions, not of individuals as individuals. These conditions are reduced to two: accumulated labour or private property, and actual labour. If both or one of these ceases, then intercourse comes to a standstill. The modern economists themselves, e.g. Sismondi, Cherbuliez, etc., oppose " association of individuals " to " association of capital." On the other hand, the individuals themselves are entirely determined by the division of labour and hence are brought into the most complete dependence on one another. Private property, in so far as within labour itself it is opposed to labour, evolves out of the necessity of accumulation, and has still, to begin with, rather the form of the community; but in its further development it approaches more and more the modern form of private property. The division of labour implies from the outset the division of the *conditions of labour*, of tools and materials, and thus the splitting up of accumulated capital among different owners, and thus, also, the division between capital and labour, and the different forms of property itself. The more the division of labour develops and accumulation grows, the sharper are the forms that this process of differentiation assumes. Labour itself can only exist on the premise of this fragmentation.

Thus two facts are here revealed. First the productive forces appear as a world for themselves, quite independent of and divorced from the individuals, alongside the individuals: the reason for this is that the individuals, whose forces they are, exist split up and in opposition to one another, whilst on the other hand these forces are only real forces in the intercourse and association of these individuals. Thus, on the one hand, we have a totality of productive forces, which have, as it were, taken on a material form and are for the individuals no longer the forces of the individuals but of private property, and hence of the individuals only in so far as they are owners of private property themselves. Never, in any earlier period, have the productive forces taken on a form so indifferent to the intercourse of individuals *as* individuals, because their intercourse itself was formerly a restricted one. On the other hand, standing over against these productive forces, we have the majority of the individuals from whom these forces have been wrested away, and who, robbed thus of all real life-content, have become abstract individuals, but who are, however, only by this fact put into a position to enter into relation with one another *as individuals*.

The only connection which still links them with the productive forces and with their own existence—labour—has lost all semblance of self-activity[43] and only sustains their life by stunting it. While in the earlier periods self-activity and the production of material life were separated, in that they devolved on different persons, and while, on account of the narrowness of the individuals themselves, the production of material life was considered as a subordinate mode of self-activity, they now diverge to such an extent that finally material life appears as the end, and what produces this material life, labour, (which is now the only possible but, as we see, negative form of self-activity), as the means.

Thus things have now come to such a pass, that the individuals must appropriate the existing totality of productive forces, not only to achieve self-activity, but, also, merely to safeguard their very existence. This appropriation is first determined by the object to be appropriated, the productive forces, which have been developed to a totality and which only exist within a universal intercourse. From this aspect alone, therefore, this appropriation must have a universal character corresponding to the productive powers and the intercourse. The appropriation of these powers is itself nothing more than the development of the individual capacities corresponding to the material instruments of production. The appropriation of a totality of instruments of production is, for this very reason, the development of a totality of capacities in the individuals themselves.

This appropriation is further determined by the persons appropriating. Only the proletarians of the present day, who are completely shut off from all self-activity, are in a position to achieve a complete and no longer restricted self-activity, which consists in the appropriation of a totality of productive forces and in the thus postulated development of a totality of capacities. All earlier revolutionary appropriations were restricted; individuals, whose self-activity was restricted by a crude instrument of production and a limited intercourse, appropriated this crude instrument of production, and hence merely achieved a new state of limitation. Their instrument of production became their property, but they themselves remained determined by the division of labour and their own instrument of production. In all expropriations up to now, a mass of individuals remained subservient to a single instrument of production; in the appropriation by the proletarians, a mass of instruments of production must be made subject to each individual, and property to all. Modern universal intercourse can be controlled by individuals, therefore, only when controlled by all.

This appropriation is further determined by the manner in which it must be effected. It can only be effected through a union, which by the character of the proletariat itself can again only be a universal one, and through a revolution, in which on the one hand the power of the earlier mode of production and intercourse and social organization is overthrown, and on the other hand there develops the universal character and the energy of the proletariat, without which the revolution cannot be accomplished; and in which, further, the proletariat rids itself of everything that still clings to it from its previous position in society.

Only at this stage does self-activity coincide with material life, which corresponds to the development of individuals into complete individuals and the casting-off of all natural limitations.⁴⁴ The transformation of labour into self-activity corresponds to the transformation of the earlier limited intercourse into the intercourse of individuals as such. With the appropriation of the total productive forces through united individuals, private property comes to an end. Whilst previously in history a particular condition always appeared as accidental, now the isolation of individuals and the particular private gain of each man have themselves become accidental.

The individuals, who are no longer subject to the division of labour, have been conceived by the philosophers as an ideal, under the name " man." They have conceived the whole process which we have outlined as the evolutionary process of "man," so that at every historical stage "man" was substituted for the individuals and shown as the motive force of history. The whole process was thus conceived as a process of the self-estrangement of " man,"⁴⁵ and this was essentially due to the fact that the average individual of the later stage was always foisted on to the earlier stage, and the consciousness of a later age on to the individuals of an earlier. Through this inversion, which from the first is an abstract image of the actual conditions, it was possible to transform the whole of history into an evolutionary process of consciousness.

·　·　·　·　·

Finally, from the conception of history we have sketched we obtain these further conclusions : (1) In the development of productive forces there comes a stage at which productive forces and means of intercourse are called into existence, which, under the existing relationships, only cause mischief, and which are no longer productive but destructive forces (machinery and money); and connected with this a class is called forth, which has to bear all the burdens of society without enjoying its advantages, which, ousted from society, is forced into the most decided antagonism to all other classes ; a class which forms the majority of all members of society, and from which emanates the consciousness of the necessity of a fundamental revolution, the communist consciousness, which may, of course, arise among the other classes too through the contemplation of the situation of this class. (2) The conditions under which definite productive forces can be applied, are the conditions of the rule of a definite class of society, whose social power, deriving from its property, has its practical-idealistic expression in each case in the form of the State ; and, therefore, every revolutionary struggle is directed against a class, which till then has been in ... er. (3) In all revolutions up till now the mode of activity always remained unscathed and it was only a question of a different distribution of this activity, a new distribution of labour to other persons, whilst the communistic revolution is directed against the preceding *mode* of activity, does away with *labour,* and abolishes the rule of all classes with the classes themselves, because it is carried through by the class which no longer counts as a class in society, is not recognized as a class, and is in itself the expression of the dissolution of all classes, nationalities, etc., within present society ; and (4) Both for the production on a mass scale of this communist consciousness, and for the success of the cause itself, the alteration of men on a mass scale is necessary, an alteration which can only take place in a practical movement, a *revolution* ; this revolution is necessary, therefore, not only because the ruling class cannot be overthrown in any other way, but also because the class *overthrowing* it can only in a revolution succeed in ridding itself of all the muck of ages and become fitted to found society anew.[46]

3. COMMUNISM: THE PRODUCTION OF THE FORM OF INTERCOURSE ITSELF.

Communism differs from all previous movements in that it overturns the basis of all earlier relations of production and intercourse, and for the first time consciously treats all natural premises as the creatures of men, strips them of their natural character and subjugates them to the power of individuals united. Its organization is, therefore, essentially economic, the material production of the conditions of this unity; it turns existing conditions into conditions of unity. The reality, which communism is creating, is precisely the real basis for rendering it impossible that anything should exist independently of individuals, in so far as things are only a product of the preceding intercourse of individuals themselves. Thus the communists in practice treat the conditions created by production and intercourse as inorganic conditions, without, however, imagining that it was the plan or the destiny of previous generations to give them material, and without believing that these conditions were inorganic for the individuals creating them.

The difference between the individual as a person and what is accidental to him, is not a conceptual difference but a historical fact. This distinction has a different significance at different times—e.g. the estate as something accidental to the individual in the eighteenth century, the family more or less too. It is not a distinction that we have to make for each age, but one which each age makes itself from among the different elements which it finds in existence, and indeed not according to any theory, but compelled by material collisions in life. Of the elements handed down to a later age from an earlier, what appears accidental to the later age as opposed to the earlier, is a form of intercourse which corresponded to a less developed stage of the productive forces. The relation of the productive forces to the form of intercourse is the relation of the form of intercourse to the occupation or activity of the individuals. (The fundamental form of this activity is, of course, material, from which depend all other forms—mental, political, religious, etc. The various shaping of material life is, of course, in every case dependent on the needs which are already developed, and both the production and the satisfaction of these needs is an historical process, which is not found in the case of a sheep or a dog [perversity of Stirner's principal argument *adversus hominem*],[47] although sheep and dogs in their present form certainly, but *malgré eux*,[48] are products of an historical process.) The conditions under which individuals have intercourse with each other, so long as the above-mentioned contradiction is absent, are conditions appertaining to their individuality, in no way external to them; conditions under which these definite individuals, living under definite relationships, can alone produce their material life and what is connected with it; are thus the conditions of their self-activity and are produced by this self-activity. The definite condition under which they produce, thus corresponds, as long as the contradiction has not yet appeared, to the reality of their conditioned nature, their one-sided existence, the one-sidedness of which only becomes evident when the contradiction enters on the scene and thus only exists for the later individuals. Then this condition appears as an accidental fetter, and the consciousness that it is a fetter is imputed to the earlier age as well.

These various conditions, which appear first as conditions of self-activity, later as fetters upon it, form in the whole evolution of history a coherent series of forms of intercourse, the coherence of which consists in this: that in the place of an earlier form of intercourse, which has become a fetter, a new one is put, corresponding to the more developed productive forces and, hence, to the advanced mode of the self-activity of individuals—a form which in its turn becomes a fetter and is then replaced by another. Since these conditions correspond at every stage to the simultaneous development of the productive forces, their history is at the same time the history of the evolving productive forces taken over by each new generation, and is therefore the history of the development of the forces of the individuals themselves.

Since this evolution takes place naturally,[49] i.e. is not subordinated to a general plan of freely combined individuals, it proceeds from various localities, tribes, nations, branches of labour, etc., each of which to start with develops independently of the others and only gradually enters into relation with the others. Furthermore, it takes place only very slowly; the various stages and interests are never completely overcome, but only subordinated to the interest of the victor, and trail along beside the latter for centuries afterwards. It follows from this that within a nation itself the individuals, even apart from their pecuniary circumstances, have quite different developments, and that an earlier interest, the peculiar form of intercourse of which has already been ousted by that belonging to a later interest, remains for a long time afterwards in possession of a traditional power in the illusory community (State, law), which has won an existence independent of the individuals; a power which in the last resort can only be broken by a revolution. This explains why, with reference to individual points which allow of a more general summing-up, consciousness can sometimes appear further advanced than the contemporary empirical relationships, so that in the struggles of a later epoch one can refer to earlier theoreticians as authorities.

On the other hand, in countries which, like North America, begin in an already advanced historical epoch, their development proceeds very rapidly. Such countries have no other natural premises than the individuals, who settled there and were led to do so because the forms of intercourse of the old countries did not correspond to their wants. Thus they begin with the most advanced individuals of the old countries, and therefore with the correspondingly most advanced form of intercourse, before this form of intercourse has been able to establish itself in the old countries.\* This is the case with all colonies, in so far as they are not mere military or trading stations. Carthage, the Greek colonies, and Iceland in the eleventh and twelfth centuries, provide examples of this. A similar relationship issues from conquest, when a form of intercourse which has evolved on another soil is brought over complete to the conquered country: whereas in its home it was still encumbered with interests and relationships left over from earlier periods, here it can and must be established completely and without hindrance, if only to assure the conquerors' lasting power. (England and Naples after the Norman Conquest, when they received the most perfect form of feudal organization.)

Thus all collisions in history have their origin, according to our view, in the contradiction between the productive forces and the form of intercourse. But also, to lead to collisions in a country, this contradiction need not necessarily come to a head in this particular country. The competition with industrially more advanced countries, brought about by the expansion of international intercourse, is sufficient to produce a

---

\*Personal energy of the individuals of various nations—Germans and Americans—energy merely through cross-breeding—hence the cretinism of the Germans—in France and England, etc., foreign peoples transplanted to an already developed soil, in America to an entirely new soil—in Germany the natural population quietly stayed where it was.

similar contradiction in countries with a backward industry (e.g. the latent proletariat in Germany brought into view by the competition of English industry).

This contradiction between the productive forces and the form of intercourse, which, as we saw, has occurred several times in past history, without however endangering its basis, necessarily on each occasion burst out in a revolution, taking on at the same time various subsidiary forms, such as all-embracing collisions, collisions of various classes, contradiction of consciousness, battle of ideas, etc., political conflict, etc. From a narrow point of view one may isolate one of these subsidiary forms and consider it as the basis of these revolutions; and this is all the more easy as the individuals who started the revolutions made illusions about their own activity according to their degree of culture and the stage of historical development.

The transformation, through the division of labour, of personal powers (relationships) into material powers, cannot be dispelled by dismissing the general idea of it from one's mind, but only by the action of individuals in again subjecting these material powers to themselves and abolishing the division of labour. This is not possible without the community. Only in community with others has each individual the means of cultivating his gifts in all directions; only in the community, therefore, is personal freedom possible. In the previous substitutes for the community, in the State, etc., personal freedom has existed only for the individuals who developed within the relationships of the ruling class, and only in so far as they were individuals of this class. The illusory community, in which individuals have up till now combined, always took on an independent existence in relation to them, and was at the same time, since it was the combination of one class over against another, not only a completely illusory community, but a new fetter as well. In the real community the individuals obtain their freedom in and through their association.

It follows from all we have been saying up till now that the communal relationship into which the individuals of a class entered, and which was determined by their common interests over against a third party, was always a community to which these individuals belonged only as average individuals, only in so far as they lived within the conditions of existence of their class—a relationship in which they participated not as individuals but as members of a class. With the community of revolutionary proletarians on the other hand, who take their conditions of existence and those of all members of society under their control, it is just the reverse; it is as individuals that the individuals participate in it. It is just this combination of individuals (assuming the advanced stage of modern productive forces, of course) which puts the conditions of the free development and movement of individuals under their control—conditions which were previously abandoned to chance and had won an independent existence over against the separate individuals just because of their separation as individuals, and because their combination had been determined by the division of labour, and through their separation had become a bond alien to them. Combination up till now (by no means an arbitrary one, such as is expounded for example in the *Contrat Social*,[50] but a necessary one) was permitted only upon these conditions, within which the individuals were at the mercy of chance (compare, e.g. the formation of the North American State and the South American republics). This right to the undisturbed enjoyment, upon certain conditions,. of fortuity and chance has up till now been called personal freedom: but these conditions are, of course, only the productive forces and forms of intercourse at any particular time.

If from a philosophical point of view one considers this evolution of individuals in the common conditions of existence of estates and classes, which followed on one another, and in the accompanying general conceptions forced upon them, it is certainly very easy to imagine that in these individuals the species, or "man", has evolved, or that they evolved " man "—and in this way one can give history some hard clouts on the ear.* One can conceive these various estates and classes to be specific terms of the general expression, subordinate varieties of the species, or evolutionary phases of " man."

This subsuming of individuals under definite classes cannot be abolished until a class has taken shape, which has no longer any particular class interest to assert against the ruling class.

Individuals have always built on themselves, but naturally on themselves within their given historical conditions and relationships, not on the " pure " individual in the sense of the ideologists. But in the course of historical evolution, and precisely through the inevitable fact that within the division of labour social relationships take on an independent existence, there appears a division within the life of each individual, in so far as it is personal and in so far as it is determined by some branch of labour and the conditions pertaining to it. (We do not mean it to be understood from this that, for example, the rentier, the capitalist, etc., cease to be persons ; but their personality is conditioned and determined by quite definite class relationships, and the division appears only in their opposition to another class and, for themselves, only when they go bankrupt.)

*The statement which frequently occurs with Saint Max (Stirner), that each is all that he is through the State, is fundamentally the same as the statement that the bourgeois is only a specimen of the bourgeois species ; a statement which presupposes that the *class* of bourgeois existed before the individuals constituting it.

In the estate (and even more in the tribe) this is as yet concealed : for instance a nobleman always remains a nobleman, a commoner always a commoner, apart from his other relationships, a quality inseparable from his individuality. The division between the personal and the class individual, the accidental nature of the conditions of life for the individual, appears only with the emergence of class, which is itself a product of the bourgeoisie. This accidental character is only engendered and developed by competition and the struggle of individuals among themselves. Thus, in imagination, individuals seem freer under the dominance of the bourgeoisie than before, because their conditions of life seem accidental ; in reality, of course, they are less free, because they are more subjected to the violence of things. The difference from the estate comes out particularly in the antagonism between the bourgeoisie and the proletariat. When the estate of the urban burghers, the corporations, etc., emerged in opposition to the landed nobility, their condition of existence—movable property and craft labour, which had already existed latently before their separation from the feudal ties—appeared as something positive, which was asserted against feudal landed property, and therefore in its own way at first took on a feudal form. Certainly the refugee serfs treated their previous servitude as something accidental to their personality. But here they only were doing what every class that is freeing itself from a fetter does ; and they did not free themselves as a class but separately. Moreover, they did not rise above the system of estates, but only formed a new estate, retaining their previous mode of labour even in their new situation, and developing it further by freeing it from its earlier fetters, which no longer corresponded to the development already attained.*

---

*N.B.—It must not be forgotten that the serfs' very need of existing and the impossibility of a large-sized economy, which involved the

For the proletarians, on the other hand, the condition of their existence, labour, and with it all the conditions of existence governing modern society, have become something accidental, something over which they, as separate individuals, have no control, and over which no *social* organization can give them control. The contradiction between the individuality of each separate proletarian and labour, the condition of life forced upon him, becomes evident to him himself, for he is sacrificed from youth upwards and, within his own class, has no chance of arriving at the conditions which would place him in the other class. Thus, while the refugee serfs only wished to be free to develop and assert those conditions of existence which were already there, and hence, in the end, only arrived at free labour, the proletarians, if they are to assert themselves as individuals, will have to abolish the very condition of their existence hitherto (which has, moreover, been that of all society up to the present), namely, labour. Thus they find themselves directly opposed to the form in which, hitherto, individuals have given themselves collective expression, that is, the State. In order, therefore, to assert themselves as individuals, they must overthrow the State.

---

distribution of the allotments among the serfs, very soon reduced the services of the serfs to their lord to an average of payments in kind and statute-labour. This made it possible for the serf to accumulate movable property and hence facilitated his escape out of the possession of his lord and gave him the prospect of prospering as an urban citizen; it also created gradations among the peasants, so that the runaway serfs were already half burghers. It is likewise obvious that the serfs who were masters of a craft had the best chance of acquiring movable property.

## TRUE SOCIALISM

THE relation between German Socialism and the proletarian movement in France and England is the same as that which we found in our first volume (cf. " Saint Max," " political liberalism ") between German liberalism, as it has hitherto existed, and the movement of the French and English bourgeoisie[1]. A number of writers have sprung up alongside the German communists, who have absorbed one or two French and English communist ideas and reinvigorated them with their own German-philosophical premises. These " socialists " or " true socialists," as they call themselves, consider foreign communist literature not as the expression and the product of a real movement but merely as a set of theoretical writings ; it has been evolved, they imagine, by a process of " pure thought," after the fashion of the German philosophical systems. It never occurs to them that, even when these writings do preach a system, they spring from the practical needs, the whole conditions of life of a particular class in particular countries. They innocently share the illusion, cherished by many such literary party representatives, that they are concerned with the " most reasonable " social order instead of with the needs of a particular class and time. The real state of affairs escapes these " true socialists," steeped as they are in their German ideology. All that they do when faced with the "unscientific " French and English is to hold up especially the superficiality and the " crude " empiricism of these foreigners to the scorn of the German public ; or else they hymn the praise of " German science " and its mission, and reveal for the first time the *truth* of communism and socialism, of absolute, *true* socialism. Moreover, as representatives of "German science" they immediately set about discharging this mission, although they are in most cases as little familiar with "German science" as they are with the original writings of the French and English, which they know only from the compilations of Stein, Oelckers, etc. And what is the "truth" which they impart to socialism and communism? Partly by reason of their ignorance of actual literary connections, partly on account of their above-mentioned misunderstanding of socialist and communist literature, they find the ideas contained in this literature quite inexplicable; they therefore attempt to clarify them by invoking the German ideology and notably that of Hegel and Feuerbach. They detach the communist systems, criticism and polemical writings from the real movement, of which they are but the expression, and force them into an arbitrary connection with German philosophy. They detach the consciousness of certain historically conditioned spheres of life from these spheres and evaluate it in terms of true, absolute, i.e. German, philosophical consciousness. With perfect consistency they transform the relations of these particular individuals into "*human*" relations; they interpret the thoughts of these particular individuals concerning their own relations as thoughts about "*mankind.*" In so doing, they have abandoned the realm of real history for the realm of ideology, and since they are ignorant of the real connection, they can now fabricate some fantastic relationship with the help of the "absolute" or some other ideological method. This translation of French ideas into the speech of the German ideologists and this arbitrarily constructed relationship between communism and German ideology form, then, the foundation of so-called "true socialism," which is loudly proclaimed, in the terms used by the Tories for the English constitution, to be "the pride of our nation and the envy of our neighbours."

"True socialism" is, then, nothing but the transfiguration of proletarian communism, and of its related parties and sects in France and England, within the heaven of the German mind and, as we shall also see, of the German temperament. "True socialism," which claims to be based on "science," is in actual fact merely another esoteric science; its theoretical literature is only for the Few who are initiated into the mysteries of the "thinking mind." But it has an exoteric literature as well; the very fact that it is concerned with social exoteric circumstances means that it must carry on some form of propaganda. In this exoteric literature it no longer appeals to the German "thinking mind" but to the German "temperament." This is all the easier since true socialism, concerned no longer with real human beings but with "man," has lost all revolutionary enthusiasm and proclaims instead the universal love of mankind. It turns as a result not to the proletarians but to the two most numerous classes of men in Germany, to the petty bourgeoisie with its philanthropic illusions and to its ideologists, the philosophers and their disciples; it turns, in short, to that "common", or uncommon, consciousness which at present rules in Germany.

The formation of this hybrid sect, and the attempt to reconcile communism with the ideas prevailing at the time, were necessary consequences of the actual conditions in Germany. The fact that a number of German communists, proceeding from a philosophical standpoint, should have arrived at communism by this path was as necessary as the fact that others, unable to extricate themselves from their ideology, should go on preaching true socialism to the bitter end. We have, therefore, no means of knowing whether those "true socialists", who wrote what we are criticizing some time ago, still maintain their position or whether they have advanced beyond it. We have, of course, no personal quarrel with them at all; we are merely considering the printed evidence of a tendency which is inevitable in a country so stagnant as Germany.

But it must not be forgotten that in addition to this, a host of young German literary men, quacks and quill-drivers of all sorts, have used the opening provided by true socialism to exploit the social movement. The lack of any *real*, passionate, practical party conflict in Germany meant that even the social movement was at first a *merely* literary one. True socialism is a perfect example of a social literary movement; its growth was not determined by any real party interests and now, after the formation of the communist party, it intends to persist in its despite. It is only to be expected that since the appearance of a real communist party in Germany, the true socialists will limit their public more and more to the petty bourgeoisie and the broken-down literary hacks who represent it.

1. *The Rhenish Annals,* or The Philosophy of True Socialism.

(a) " *Communism, Socialism, Humanism.*"[2]

We begin with this essay because it displays perfectly consciously and with great complacency the national German character of true socialism.

> The French seem to have misunderstood their own men of genius. German science comes to their aid at this point, presenting in socialism the most reasonable social order, if one can speak of a superlative degree of reasonableness!

" German science " presents, therefore, a social order, in fact " the most reasonable social order " " in socialism." Socialism is reduced to a branch of that omnipotent, omniscient, all-embracing German science which is actually capable of founding a society. It is true that socialism is French in origin, but the French socialists were " essentially " Germans, for which reason the real Frenchmen did not understand them. Thus the writer can state:

> Communism is French, socialism is German; the French are lucky to possess so keen a social instinct; it will serve them one day as a substitute for scientific investigation. This could have been anticipated from the evolution of the two nations; the French arrived at communism by way of politics [now we know of course, how the French came to communism] the Germans arrived at socialism [namely "true socialism"] by way of metaphysics, which eventually changed into anthropology.[3] Ultimately both are resolved in humanism.

After you have transformed communism and socialism into two abstract theories, two principles, there is, of course, nothing easier than to excogitate any Hegelian unity you please from these two opposites and to give it any vague name you choose. You have thereby not only submitted " the evolution of the two nations " to a piercing scrutiny but you have also brilliantly demonstrated the superiority of the speculative individual over both Frenchmen and Germans. Incidentally, the sentence is copied more or less literally from Püttmann's *Bürgerbuch,* page 43 and elsewhere; the writer's "scientific investigation" of socialism is likewise limited to a reproduction, in a new arrangement, of the ideas contained in this book, in the *Einundzwanzig Bogen* and in other writings dating from the early days of German communism.

We will only give a few examples of the objections raised to communism in this essay:

> Communism does not combine the atoms into an organic whole.

The combination of " atoms " into an " organic whole " is just as little to be desired as the squaring of the circle.

> Communism, in its main centre, France, takes the form of crude opposition to the self-centred disintegration of the commercial State ; it never transcends this political opposition ; it never rises to the concept of unconditioned, absolute freedom.

There you have the German-ideological postulate of "unconditioned absolute freedom" which must be "taken for granted," which is only the practical formula for "unconditioned absolute thought." French communism is admittedly "crude" because it is the theoretical expression of a *real* opposition ; but the writer suggests that the only way to transcend this opposition is to imagine it to be already overcome. Compare by the by, *Bürgerbuch*, page 43, etc.

> Tyranny can perfectly well persist under communism, since the latter refuses to permit the continuance of the genus.

Hapless genus ! " Genus " and " tyranny " have hitherto co-existed ; but communism allows tyranny to persist just because it abolishes the " genus." And how, according to our true socialists, does communism set about abolishing the " genus ? " It " only has the masses in view."

> In communism man is not conscious of his essence ... his dependence is reduced by communism to the lowest, most brutal relationship, to dependence on crude matter—the separation of labour and enjoyment. Man does not attain to free moral activity.

In order to appreciate the " scientific investigation " which has led our true socialist to this proposition, we should compare the following one :

## TRUE SOCIALISM

French socialists and communists have no theoretical understanding whatsoever of the essence of socialism—even the radical (French) communists are still unable to transcend the antithesis of labour and enjoyment . . . have not yet risen to the idea of free activity. . . . The only difference between communism and the commercial world is that in communism the complete alienation of real human property is to be in no way fortuitous, i.e. is to be idealized. (*Bürgerbuch*, page 43.)

That is to say, our true socialist is reproaching the French for having a correct consciousness of their actual social conditions, instead of bringing to light " man's " consciousness of " his essence." All that these true socialists have against the French amounts to this, that their movement as a whole does not consider Feuerbach's philosophy to be the last word. The writer proceeds in reality from the postulate of the separation of labour and enjoyment. Instead of dealing with this postulate, he ideologically turns the whole thing upside down, starts with the missing consciousness of man, deduces from it his " dependence on crude matter " and assumes this to be realized in the " separation of labour and enjoyment." But we shall see later on where our true socialist gets to with his independence " of crude matter." As a matter of fact, these gentlemen display a remarkable delicacy of feeling. Everything shocks them, especially matter; they complain everywhere of crudity. We have already had a "crude antithesis"; now we have "the most brutal relationship" of "dependence on crude matter."

> With gaping jaws the German cries:
> Too crude love must not be
> Or you'll get an infirmity.[4]

German philosophy in its socialist disguise appears, of course, to investigate " crude reality," but it always keeps at a respectable distance; it cries, in hysterical and irritable tones: *noli me tangere* !⁵

After these scientific objections to French communism, we come to a discussion of some historical questions. This is a brilliant exposition of the " free moral activity " and " scientific investigation " of our true socialist and of his independence of crude matter.

On page 170 he arrives at the " result " that the only communism which exists is " crude French communism " (crude once again). The construction of this truth *a priori* is carried out with great " social instinct " and shows that " man has become conscious of his essence." Listen to this:

> There is no other communism, for (!) what Weitling has produced is only an elaboration of the ideas which he learnt in Paris and Geneva from Fourier and the Communists.

" There is no " English communism for " what Weitling," etc.! Thomas More, the Levellers, Owen, Thompson, Watts, Holyoake, Harney, Morgan, Southwell, Goodwin Barmby, Greaves, Edmonds, Hobson, Spence will be amazed, or respectively turn in their graves, when they hear that they are no communists " because " Weitling went to Paris and Geneva.

Moreover, Weitling's communism does seem to be different in kind from the " crude French " variety, in vulgar parlance, from Babœufism, since it contains some of " Fourier's ideas " as well.

> The communists were particularly given to drawing up systems or ready-made social orders (Cabet's Icarie, la Félicité,⁶, Weitling). All systems are, however, dogmatic and dictatorial.

By this verdict on systems in general true socialism has, of course, saved itself the trouble of acquainting itself at first hand with the communist systems. With one blow it has overthrown not only Icarie but also every philosophical system from Aristotle to Hegel, the *Système de la nature*,[7] the botanical system of Linnæus and Jussieu and even the solar system. As a matter of fact one need only point out that the systems themselves nearly all appeared in the early days of the communist movement; they had at that time propaganda value as popular novels, which corresponded perfectly to the undeveloped consciousness of the proletarians, who were then just getting into their stride. Cabet himself calls his Icarie a " philosophic novel " ; he must on no account be judged by his system but rather by his polemical writings, in fact his whole activity as a party leader. In some of these novels, e.g. Fourier's system, there is a vein of true poetry ; others, like the systems of Owen and Cabet, show not a shred of imagination and are written in a business-like calculating way or else with an eye to the views of the class to be influenced, in the slyest lawyer fashion. As the party develops, these systems lose all importance and are at best retained purely nominally as catchwords. Who in France believes in Icarie, who in England believes in the plans of Owen, which he preached in various modifications with an eye to propaganda among particular classes or with respect to the altered circumstances of the moment ? Fourier's orthodox disciples of the *Démocratie pacifique*[8] show most clearly how little the real content of these systems lies in their systematic form ; they are, for all their orthodoxy, doctrinaire bourgeois, the very antipodes of Fourier. All epoch-making systems have as their real content the needs of the time in which they arose. Each one of them is based on the whole of the antecedent development of a nation, on the historical growth of its class relations with their political, moral, philosophical and other consequences. The assertion that all systems are dogmatic, dictatorial is of no significance for this basis and this content of the communist systems. The Germans had not, like the English and the French, a society of fully developed class relations before them. The German communists could only base their systems on the relations of the class from which they sprang. It is, therefore, perfectly natural that the only existing German communist system should be a reproduction of French ideas in terms of a mental outlook which was limited by the petty circumstances of the artisan class.

" The folly of Cabet, who insists that everyone should subscribe to his *Populaire* "[9] is proof of the tyranny that persists within communism. Our friend takes the claims which a party leader makes on his party, impelled by particular circumstances and the danger of dissipating limited financial means ; he first of all distorts them and then evaluates them in terms of the " essence of man." Of course he is bound to conclude that this party leader and all other partisans are " foolish," whereas purely disinterested figures, like himself and the " essence of man," are of sound intellect. But let him find out the true state of affairs from Cabet's *Ma ligne droite*.

Finally, the whole antithesis of our author, and of German true socialists and ideologists in general, to the real movements of other nations is epitomized in one classic sentence. The Germans judge everything *sub specie æterni* (in terms of the essence of man), foreigners view everything practically, in terms of actually existing men and circumstances. The thoughts and actions of the foreigner are temporal, the thoughts and actions of the German are timeless. Our true socialist confesses this as follows :

> The very name of communism, the contrary of competition, reveals its one-sidedness ; but is this bias, which no doubt carries some weight now as a party name, to last for ever ?

After having thus thoroughly disposed of communism, the writer proceeds to its contrary, *socialism*. "Socialism establishes that anarchic order of things which is essentially peculiar to the human race and to the universe"— the reason, no doubt, why it has hitherto never existed for "the human race." Free competition is too "crude" to appear to our true socialist as an "anarchic order of things."

Socialism, "fully confident in the moral core of mankind," decrees that " the union of the sexes is and should be merely the highest intensification of love ; for only what is natural is true and what is true is moral."

The reason why " the union, etc., etc., is and should be " is one which could be applied to everything. For example, " socialism, fully confident in the moral core " of the apes, might just as well decree that the masturbation which occurs naturally among them is, and should be, merely the highest intensification of " self "-love ; " for only what is natural is true and what is true is moral."

It would be hard to say by what standard socialism judges what is " natural."

> Activity and enjoyment coincide in the peculiar nature of man ; they are determined by the latter and not by the products external to us.
> But since these products are indispensable for activity, that is to say for true life, and since by reason of the common activity of mankind they have, so to speak, detached themselves from mankind, they are or should be the common substratum of further development for all (community of goods).
> Present-day society is indeed barbarous ; certain individuals fall upon the products of another's labour with beastly voracity and themselves relapse into an idleness which corrupts their own essence (rentiers[10]) ; as a necessary consequence, others are driven to mechanical forms of production ; their property

(their own human essence) has been impoverished, not by idleness, but by galling exertion (proletarians). ... The two extremes of our society, rentiers and proletarians, are, however, at the same stage of development. Both are dependent upon things external to them [or are negroes, as Saint Max would say.]

True socialism has never " detached from itself, as a product indispensable to true life," anything more perfect than the results reached above by our " Mongol " concerning " our savagery "; he believes that " all mankind " is bound to " fall upon them " with " beastly voracity " by reason of its " peculiar nature."

The four ideas—" rentiers," " proletarians," " mechanical " and " community of goods "—are for our Mongol at any rate " products external to him "; as far as they are concerned, his " activity " and his " enjoyment " consist in representing them as anticipated terms for the results of his own " mechanical form of production."

Civilization, we learn has relapsed into savagery and consequently the individuals who actually form society suffer from all kinds of infirmities. Society is abstracted from these individuals, it is made independent, it relapses into savagery on its own, and the individual suffers only as a result of this relapse. The terms— beast of prey, idle, possessor of a corrupt nature —are the first result of this relapse; they define, we learn to our horror, the " rentiers." The only comment necessary is that this " corruption of their own essence " is nothing but a form of words invented by our puzzled philosopher in his endeavour to understand " idleness," the practical components of which seem but little known.

The two terms, "impoverishment of their own human essence by galling exertion " and " being driven to mechanical forms of production ", are the second "necessary consequence " of this primary result of the relapse into savagery. They are a "necessary consequence of the corruption of the rentiers' essence" and are known in vulgar parlance, we learn, once more to our horror, as "the proletarian."

The following sequence of cause and effect occurs, therefore: It is a fact that proletarians exist and that they work mechanically. Why are proletarians driven to "mechanical forms of production?" Because of the corrupt essence of the rentiers. Why is the essence of the rentier corrupt? Because "present-day society is so barbarous." Why is it so barbarous? Ask thy Maker.

Characteristically, our true socialist sees "the extremes of *our* society" in the opposition of rentiers and proletarians. This opposition has been present in one form or another at all fairly highly advanced stages of society and has been belaboured by all moralists since time immemorial; it was resurrected right at the beginning of the proletarian movement at a time when the proletariat still had interests in common with the industrial and petty bourgeoisie. Compare, for example, the writings of Cobbett and P. L. Courrier or Saint-Simon, who originally numbered the industrial capitalists among his "workers" as opposed to his "idlers," the rentiers. Here we have an example of what German scientific thoroughness (perfected as it is in true socialism) always amounts to in practice. It defines this trivial antithesis, and then goes on to clothe it, not in the language of ordinary men, but in the sacred language of philosophy; it chooses abstract, sanctified and quite inappropriate terms to express its childish discovery. The conclusion puts the finishing touch to such thoroughness. Our true socialist merges the totally dissimilar stages of development of the proletarians and the rentiers into "one and the same stage of development"; he is enabled to do so by ignoring their real stages of development and by subsuming them under the philosophic phrase: " dependence upon things external to them." True socialism has here discovered the stage of development at which the dissimilarity of all such stages in the three realms of nature, geology and history, vanishes into thin air.

Although he detests " dependence upon things external to him," our true socialist nevertheless admits that he is dependent upon them, " since products," i.e. these very things, " are indispensable to activity " and to " true life." He makes this shame-faced confession so that he can clear the road for a philosophical construction—the community of goods—the absurdity of which will be immediately apparent to the reader.

We now come to the first of the passages quoted above. Here again, " independence from things " is claimed in respect of activity and enjoyment. Activity and enjoyment " are conditioned " by " the peculiar nature of man." If he had demonstrated this peculiar nature in the activity and enjoyment of the men who surround him, he would very soon have found how far the products external to us have a voice in the matter, too ; but instead, he states that both activity and enjoyment " coincide in the peculiar nature of man." Instead of visualizing the peculiar nature of men in their activity and their manner of enjoyment, which is conditioned by their activity, he explains both by invoking " the peculiar nature of man," which cuts short any further discussion. He abandons the real behaviour of the individual and takes refuge in his indescribable, inaccessible, peculiar nature. We see here, moreover, what the true socialists understand by "free activity." Our author imprudently reveals to us that it is activity which " is not conditioned by things external to us," i.e. *actus purus*, pure absolute activity, which amounts in the last instance to much the same thing as the illusion of " pure thought." It naturally sullies the purity of this activity if one imputes to it a material basis and a material result; the true socialist deals only reluctantly with impure activity of this kind; he despises its product, which he terms " a mere lapse from humanity," and not " a result." The subject from whom this pure activity proceeds cannot, therefore, be a real sentient being; it can only be the thinking mind. This " free activity," with its excessively German flavour, is nothing but " unconditioned absolute freedom " in a new guise. The true socialists merely conceal their ignorance of real production by this talk of "free activity"; that it amounts in the long run to "pure thought" is shown by the fact that the writer gives us as his last word the postulate of true cognition.

> This separation of the two outstanding parties of the age [namely, French crude communism and German socialism] is a result of the developments of the last two years, which started more particularly with Hess's *Philosophy of Action;* in Herwegh's *Einundzwanzig Bogen.* It was high time to throw a little more light on the shibboleths of the social parties.

On the one hand we have the actual existing communist party in France with its literature and, on the other, a few German pseudo-scholars who are trying to elucidate the ideas of this literature philosophically. The latter are hailed just as much as the former as an " outstanding party of the age," as a party, that is to say, of infinite importance not only to its immediate antithesis, the French communists, but also to the English chartists and communists, the American national reformers and indeed to every other party " of the age." It is unfortunate that none of these know of the existence of this " outstanding party" of ours. But it has for a considerable time been the fashion among German ideologists for each literary faction, particularly the one that thinks itself " most daring," to proclaim itself not merely as an " outstanding party," but actually as " *the* outstanding party of the age." We have among others, " the outstanding party " of critical criticism, the " outstanding party " of complacent egoism and now the " outstanding party " of the true socialists. In this fashion Germany can show a whole horde of " outstanding parties " whose existence is known only in Germany and even there only among the small set of scholars, pseudo-scholars and literary hacks. They all imagine that they are weaving the web of history when, as a matter of fact, they are merely spinning the long yarn of their own imaginings.

This " outstanding party " of the true socialists is " a result of the developments of the last two years which started more particularly with the philosophy of Hess." It is " a result ", that is to say, of the developments " of the last two years " when our author first got entangled in socialism and found it was " high time " to enlighten himself " a little more " by means of a few " shibboleths," on what he considers to be " social parties."

Having thus dismissed communism and socialism, our author introduces us to the higher synthesis of the two, to humanism. From now on, we shall be in the realm of " mankind," and history in its true sense will be enacted, for our true socialist, in Germany alone.

All quibbles about names are resolved in humanism ; wherefore communists, wherefore socialists ? We are human beings—*tous frères, tous amis.*[11]

Swim not, brothers, against the stream,
That's only a useless thing !
Let us climb up on to Templow hill
And cry : God save the King ![12]

Wherefore human beings, wherefore beasts, wherefore plants, wherefore stones ? We are bodies !

## TRUE SOCIALISM

An historical dissertation follows, based upon German science; "the French will one day find a substitute for it in their social instinct." Antiquity—naivety; the Middle Ages—Romanticism; the Modern Age—Humanism. By means of these three trivialities, the writer constructs humanism historically and represents it as the truth towards which the humanities have ever striven. Compare Saint Max in the first volume for constructions of this kind; he manufactures such articles in a much more artistic and less amateurish way.

On page 172 we are informed that "the final result of scholasticism is that cleavage of life which Hess disposed of." Here then, the cause of the cleavage of life is shown to be theory. It is difficult to see why these true socialists mention society at all if they believe with the philosophers that all real cleavages are evoked by the cleavage of concepts. On the basis of the philosophical belief in the power of concepts to make or destroy the world, they can perfectly well imagine that some individual "disposed of the cleavage of life" by "disposing" in some way or other of concepts. Like all German ideologists, the true socialists continually mix up literary history and real history as equally effective. This habit is, of course, very understandable among the Germans, who conceal the abject part they have played and continue to play in real history by equating the illusions, in which they are so rich, with reality.

And now to the "last two years," during which German science has so thoroughly disposed of all problems that nothing remains to the other nations but to carry out its decrees.

> Feuerbach only partially completed, or rather only began, the task of anthropology, the regaining by man of his estranged nature [the nature of man or the nature of Feuerbach?]; he destroyed the religious

illusion, the theoretical abstraction, the God-Man, while Hess annihilates the political illusion, the abstraction of his wealth, of his activity [is he referring to Hess or to man?]; that is, he annihilates wealth. It was the work of Hess which freed man from the last of the forces external to him, and made him capable of moral activity—for all the unselfishness of earlier times [before Hess] was only an illusory unselfishness—and raised him once more to his former dignity; for was man ever previously [before Hess] esteemed for what he actually was? Was he not judged by what he possessed? He was esteemed for his money.

It is characteristic of all these high-sounding phrases about liberation, etc., that it is always " man " who is liberated. Although it would appear from the claims made above that " wealth " and " money " have ceased to exist, we nevertheless learn in the following sentence : " Now that these illusions have been destroyed " (money is, admittedly, an illusion, viewed *sub specie æterni*, *l'or n'est qu'une chimère*)[13] " we can think about a new *human* order of society." But this is surely quite superfluous since " the recognition of the essence of man has as a necessary and natural result a life which is truly human."

To arrive at communism or socialism by way of metaphysics or politics, etc., etc.—these phrases beloved of true socialists merely indicate that such and such a writer has adapted communist ideas (which have reached him from without and have arisen in circumstances quite different from his) to his own mode of expression, and has then formulated them from his own actual standpoint. Whether the standpoint of a nation is predominantly metaphysical or political, whether its outlook on communism has a political or metaphysical or any other bias depends of course upon the whole development of the nation. The fact that the attitude of most French communists has a political complexion—which might be countered by the fact that very many French socialists have abstracted completely from politics—causes our author to infer that the French " have arrived at communism by way of politics," by way of their political development. This inference, which has a very wide circulation in Germany, does not imply that the writer has any knowledge either of politics, particularly of French politics, or of communism; it only shows that he considers politics to be an independent sphere of activity, subject to an independent development, a belief which he shares with all ideologists.

Another catchword of the true socialists is " true property," " true personal property," " real," " social," " living," " natural," etc. property, whereas private property is termed by them in an extremely characteristic way, " *so-called* property." The Saint-Simonists were the first to adopt this manner of speaking, as we have already pointed out in the first volume; but they never lent it this German metaphysical-mysterious form; it was indeed justified to some extent at the beginning of the socialist movement as a counter to the stupid outcry of the bourgeoisie. The end to which most of the Saint-Simonists came shows at any rate the ease with which this " true property " can degenerate into " ordinary private property."

If one imagines the antithesis of communism to the world of private property in its crudest form, i.e. in an abstract form in which the real conditions of that antithesis are ignored, then one is faced with the antithesis of property and lack of property. The abolition of this antithesis can be viewed as the abolition of either the one side or the other; either property can be abolished in which case universal lack of property or destitution results, or else the lack of property may be abolished, which means the establishment of true property. In reality, the actual property owners stand on one side and the propertyless communist proletarians on the other. This opposition becomes keener day by day and is rapidly driving to a crisis. If then, the theoretical representatives of the proletariat wish their literary activity to have any practical result whatsoever, they must first and foremost insist that all phrases be swept aside which obscure the real sharpness of the opposition and which hush it up. Such phrases actually give the bourgeois a chance to safeguard their interests by insinuating themselves among the communists on the strength of their philanthropic enthusiasms. All these rotten qualities are, however, to be found in the catchwords of the true socialists and particularly in " true property." Of course, we realize that the communist movement cannot be destroyed by a few German phrase-mongers. Nevertheless, it is essential to resist all phrases which obscure and dilute still further the realization that communism is totally opposed to the existing world order. It is particularly necessary in a country like Germany, where philosophic phrases have for centuries exerted a certain power, and where, moreover, class divisions are not so clearly marked as in other countries, with the result that the German communists are less keenly and decisively aware of the real issues.

This theory of true property conceives *real* private property, as it has hitherto existed, merely as a semblance, whereas it views the concept abstracted from this real property as the *truth* and *reality* of the semblance; it is therefore ideological all through. All it does is to give clearer and more precise expression to the ideas of the petty bourgeois; for their benevolent endeavours and pious wishes aim likewise at the abolition of the lack of property.

In this essay we have had yet further evidence of the narrowly national outlook which underlies the alleged universalism and cosmopolitanism of the Germans.

The land belongs to the Russians and French,
The English own the sea.
But we in the airy realm of dreams
Hold sovereign mastery.

Our unity is perfect here,
Our power beyond dispute;
The other folk in solid earth
Have meanwhile taken root.[14]

With infinite complacency the Germans draw the attention of the other peoples to this airy realm of dreams, the realm of " human essence " ; it is, they claim, the consummation and the goal of all world history ; in every sphere they regard their dreamy phantasies as a final verdict on the actions of other nations ; their lot is to be everywhere onlookers and inspectors, and so they believe themselves called upon to sit in judgment on the whole world and to stand by while history works out its ultimate purpose in Germany. We have already observed several times that the complement of this inflated and extravagant national pride is practical activity of the pettiest kind, worthy of shopkeepers and artisans. National narrow-mindedness is everywhere repellent. In Germany it is positively odious, since there it is upheld in the face of those nations which openly confess their national limitations and their dependence upon real interests, the Germans cherishing the illusion that they are superior to nationality and to all real interests. It is, of course, true of every nation that insistence upon nationality is now to be found only among the bourgeoisie and their writers.

*(b) " Cornerstones of Socialism."*

In this essay the reader is first of all prepared for the weighty truths of true socialism by an elegant poetic prologue. The prologue opens by proclaiming " happiness," to be the "ultimate aim of all endeavour, all movements, of all the laborious yet untiring exertions of past epochs." In a few brief strokes, we are sketched a history of the struggle for happiness:

> When the foundations of the old world crumbled, the human heart with all its yearning took refuge in another world, to which it transferred its happiness.

Hence all the bad luck of the real world. In recent times man has bidden farewell to the other world and our true socialist now asks:

> Can man greet the earth once more as the land of his happiness? Does he once more recognize in her his original home? Why then should he still keep Life and Happiness apart? Why does he not break down the last barrier which cleaves earthly life into two hostile halves?

" Land of my most blissful feelings ! " etc.

He now invites "man" to accompany him on a journey, an invitation which "man" readily accepts. "Man" enters the realm of "free nature" and indulges, among other things, in the following intimate confessions of a true socialist.

> . ! . . gay flowers . . . tall and stately oaks . . . their satisfaction, their happiness lie in their growth and their blossoming . . . an infinite multitude of tiny creatures in the meadows . . . forest birds . . . a mettlesome troop of young horses . . . I see [it is "man" who speaks] that these creatures neither know nor desire any other happiness than that which lies for them in the expression and the enjoyment of their lives. When night falls, my eyes behold a countless host of worlds which revolve about each other in endless space according to eternal laws. I see in their revolutions a unity of life, movement and happiness.

> "Man" could observe a quantity of other things in nature, e.g. the bitterest competition among plants and

animals; he could see, for example, in the plant world, in his " forest of tall and stately oaks " how these tall and stately capitalists consume the nutriment of the tiny shrubs, which might well complain: *terra, aqua, aere et igni interdicti sumus*[15]; he could observe the parasites, the ideologists of the vegetable world, he could further observe that there is open warfare between the " forest birds " and the " infinite multitude of tiny creatures," between the grass of his " meadows " and the " mettlesome troop of young horses." He could see in his " countless host of worlds " a whole heavenly feudal monarchy complete with tenants and vassals, a few of which, e.g. the moon, lead a very poor life *aere et aqua interdicti*; a feudal system in which even the homeless vagabonds, the comets, have been apportioned their station in life and in which the shattered asteroids bear witness to occasional unpleasant scenes, while the meteors, those fallen angels, creep shamefaced through the " infinite space," until they find somewhere or other a modest lodging. In the further distance, he would come upon the reactionaries, the fixed stars.

All these beings find their happiness, the satisfaction and the enjoyment of their life in the practice and expression of the vital energies with which nature has endowed them.

That is, " man " finds from the mutual interaction of natural bodies and from the expression of their energies that it is in these that the natural bodies find their happiness, etc.

" Man " is now reproached by our true socialist with his discord :

Did not man too spring from the primeval world, is he too not a child of nature, like all other creatures ? Is he not composed of the same materials, is he not endowed with those general energies and properties which animate all things? Why does he still seek his earthly happiness in an earthly Beyond?

"Those general energies and properties" which man has in common with "all things," are cohesion, impenetrability, volume, gravity, etc., which can be found set out in detail on the first page of any text-book of physics. It is difficult to see how one can construe this as a reason why man should not "seek his happiness in an earthly Beyond." However, he admonishes man as follows:

Consider the lilies of the field.

Yes, consider the lilies of the field, how they are eaten by goats, transplanted by man into his button-hole, how they are crushed beneath the immodest embraces of the dairymaid and the donkey-driver!

Consider the lilies of the field, how they grow; they toil not, neither do they spin: and thy Heavenly Father feedeth them.

Go thou and do likewise!

After learning in this fashion of the unity of "man" with "all things," we now learn how he differs from "all things."

But man knows himself, he is conscious of himself. Whereas in other beings, the natural instincts and energies manifest themselves in isolation and unconsciously, they are united in man, he is aware of them ... his nature is the mirror of all nature, which knows itself in him. Well then! If nature recognizes herself in me, then I recognize myself in nature. I see in her life my own life.... Let us then give living expression to that with which nature has imbued us.

This whole prologue is a model of ingenuous philosophic mystification. The true socialist proceeds from the thought that the dichotomy of life and happiness must cease. To prove his statement, he summons the aid of nature and assumes that in it this dichotomy does not exist; from this he deduces that since man, too, is a natural body and possesses all the general properties of such a body, no dichotomy should exist for him either. Hobbes, also by invoking nature, produced a proof of his *bellum omnium contra omnes*[16] that is much more conclusive than Herr Grün's attempt to prove a contrary hypothesis. Hegel, whose construction[17] our true socialist uses as a starting-point, actually perceives in nature the cleavage, the dissolute period of the absolute idea and even calls the animal the concrete anguish of God. After shrouding nature in mystery, our true socialist shrouds human consciousness in mystery too, by making it the mirror of nature. Of course, when the consciousness, in expressing itself, ascribes to nature itself the expression of a pious wish about human affairs, it is self-evident that the consciousness will only be the mirror in which nature contemplates itself. "Man," it is asserted, has to abolish in his own sphere the cleavage which is assumed to be non-existent in nature; this was first proved by reference to man in his quality as a mere natural body; it is now proved by reference to him in his function of passive mirror, a mirror in which nature becomes aware of herself. But let us inspect the last sentence more closely; all the nonsense of his arguments is concentrated in it.

The first fact asserted is that man possesses self-consciousness. The instincts and energies of individual natural beings are transformed into the instincts and forces "of nature," which then, as a matter of course, are manifested in isolation in these individual beings. This mystification was needed in order later to unite these instincts and forces "of nature" artificially in the human self-consciousness. From this, it clearly follows that the self-consciousness of man can be transformed into the self-consciousness of nature within him. This mystification is apparently clarified by saying that man, in order to pay nature back for finding her self-consciousness in him, seeks his, in turn, in nature—a procedure which enables him, of course, to find nothing in her except what he imputed to her by means of the mystification described above.

He has now arrived safely at the point from which he originally started. He has turned right round on his heel—and that is what they now call in Germany ... development.

After this prologue comes the real exposition of true socialism.

### First Cornerstone

Saint-Simon said to his disciples on his death-bed:

"My whole life can be expressed in one thought: all men must be assured the freest development of their natural capacities." Saint-Simon was a herald of socialism.

This statement is now discussed according to the true socialist method described above, with an admixture of that mystification of nature which we saw in the prologue.

Nature as the basis of all life is a unity which proceeds from itself and returns to itself, which embraces the manifold variety of its phenomena and apart from which nothing exists.

We have seen how one contrives to transform the different natural bodies and their mutual relationships into manifold "phenomena" of the secret essence of this mysterious "unity." The only new factor is that nature is first called the "basis of all life," and then we are informed that "apart from it, nothing exists," which would imply that it embraces "life" as well and cannot therefore merely be its basis. After these portentous words, there follows the pivotal point of the whole essay:

> Every one of these phenomena, every individual existence, lives and develops only through its opposition to, its struggle with, the external world; is based upon its interaction with the totality of existences, with which it is in turn linked in a whole, the organic unity of the universe.

This pivotal sentence is further elucidated as follows:

> The individual existence finds on the one hand its foundation, its source and its subsistence in the totality of existence; on the other hand, the totality of existence is engaged in continual conflict with the individual life; it strives to consume and to absorb it."

Since this statement applies to every individual existence, it can be, and is, applied to men as well:

> Man can therefore only develop in and through the totality of existence (No. 1).

Conscious individual existence is now contrasted with unconscious individual existence; human society with natural life in general; and then the sentence which we quoted last is repeated in the following form:

> By reason of my nature, I can only develop, I can only attain happiness, self-conscious enjoyment of my life, in and through community with other men (No. 2).

This development of the individual in society is now discussed in the same way as "individual existence" in general was treated above:

> In society, too, the opposition of individual existence and existence in general becomes the condition of conscious human development. Only through perpetual conflict, through perpetual reaction against society which opposes me as a restricting force, do I achieve self-determination and freedom, without which there is no happiness. My life is a continuous process of liberation, a continuous battle with and

## THE GERMAN IDEOLOGY

victory over the conscious and unconscious external world, so that I may subdue it and use it to the enjoyment of my life. The instinct of self-preservation, the striving for my own happiness, freedom and satisfaction, these are therefore natural, i.e. reasonable, expressions of life.

Further:

I demand, in consequence, from society that it should afford me the possibility of winning from it my satisfaction, my happiness, that it should provide a battlefield for my bellicose desires. Just as the individual plant demands earth, warmth and sun, air and rain for its growth, so that it may bear leaves, blossoms and fruit, man too desires to find in society the conditions for the all-round development and satisfaction of all his needs, inclinations and capacities. It must offer him the possibility of winning his happiness. How he will use that chance, what he will make of himself, of his life, depends upon him, upon his individuality. I alone can determine my own happiness.

There follows, as the conclusion of the whole argument, the statement by Saint-Simon which is quoted at the beginning of this section. The Frenchman's idea has thus been vindicated by the science of the German. How does he vindicate it?

The true socialist has already imputed various ideas to nature which he would like to see realized in human society. Nature is now mirrored in society as a whole, not merely, as formerly, in the individual human being. A further conclusion can be drawn about human society from the ideas imputed to nature. Since our author does not embark upon the historical development of society, contenting himself with this sterile analogy, we have to ask ourselves why society should not always have been a true image of nature. The phrases about society, which opposes the individual in the shape of a restricting force, are therefore relevant to every form of society. It is perhaps natural that a few inconsequences should have crept into this interpretation of society but one cannot ignore the struggle which now appears in nature and which contrasts so sharply with the harmony of the prologue. Society, the "totality of existence," is conceived by our author not as the interaction of the constituent "individual existences," but as a separate existence which undergoes another and separate interaction with these "individual existences." If there is any reference to real affairs in all this it is the illusion of the independence of the State as opposed to private life and the belief in this apparent independence as something absolute. But as a matter of fact, neither here nor anywhere in the whole essay is it a question of nature and society at all; it is merely a question of the two categories, individuality and totality, which are given various names and which are said to form a contradiction, the reconciliation of which would be highly desirable.

As a result of the vindication of "individual existence" as opposed to "the totality of existence," the satisfaction of needs, the development of capacities, self-love, etc., become "natural, reasonable expressions of life." As a result of the conception of society as an image of nature, it follows that these expressions of life, in all forms of society, the present included, have attained full maturity and are recognized as justified.

But we suddenly learn on page 159 that "in our present-day society," reasonable, natural expressions of life are "so often repressed" and "only for that reason do they usually degenerate into an unnatural distortion, egoism, vice, etc."

And so, since society does not, after all, correspond to its prototype, nature, the true socialist demands that it *should* conform to nature and justifies his claim by adducing the plant as an example—a most unfortunate example. In the first place, the plant does not "demand" of nature all the conditions of existence enumerated above; unless it finds them already present it never becomes a plant at all; it remains a grain of seed. Moreover, the composition of the "leaves, blossoms and fruit" depends to a great extent on the "soil," the "warmth" and so on, the climatic and geological conditions of its growth. Far from "demanding" anything, the plant is seen to depend utterly upon the actual conditions of its existence; nevertheless, it is upon this alleged demand that our true socialist bases his own claim for a form of society which shall conform to his "individuality." The demand for a true socialist society is based on the imaginary demand of a coco-nut palm that the "totality of existence" should furnish it with "soil, warmth, sun, air and rain" at the North Pole.

This claim of the individual on society is not deduced from the real development of society but from the alleged relationship of the metaphysical categories, individuality and totality. You have only to interpret single individuals as representatives, embodiments of individuality, and society as the embodiment of totality, and the whole trick is done. And at the same time you have expressed correctly Saint-Simon's statement about the free development of the capacities; you have placed it upon a true foundation. By expressing it correctly the author means the nonsensical argument that the individuals forming society will preserve their "individuality," will remain as they are, while they demand of society a transformation which can only proceed from a transformation of themselves.

*Second Cornerstone.*

You've forgotten the rest of the charming refrain? Well, just give it up and start over again!

## TRUE SOCIALISM

> "The world organism is
> the infinite multiplicity
> of all existences
> reduced to unity."

And so we find ourselves hurled back to the beginning of the essay and have to go through the whole comedy of individual existence and totality of existence for the second time. Once more we are initiated into the deep mystery of the interaction of these two existences. But this time a new term makes its appearance: "polar relationship"; and individual existence is changed into a mere symbol, an "image" of the totality of existence. There is something kaleidoscopic about this essay; it is entirely composed of reflections of itself, a method of argument common to all true socialists. They distribute their arguments like the cherryseller who insisted on selling her wares below cost price, working on the orthodox economic principle that all that matters is the quantity sold. A necessary method for true socialism, since its cherries were rotten before they were ripe.

A few examples of this self-reflection follow:

| Cornerstone No. 1. pp., 158–9. | Cornerstone No. 2, pp. 160–1. |
|---|---|
| Every individual existence is and develops only through its opposite ... is based upon its interaction with the totality of existence. | Every individual existence is and develops in and through the totality of existence; the totality of existence only develops in and through the individual existence. (Interaction.) |
| With which it is, in turn, linked in a whole. | |
| Organic unity of the universe. | The individual existence develops ... as a part of existence in general. |
| The individual existence finds on the one hand its foundation, its source and its subsistence in the totality of existence; | The world organism consists of all individual existences unified. |
| | Which (the totality of |

I

# 110 THE GERMAN IDEOLOGY

on the other hand, the totality of existence is engaged in continual conflict with the individual life; it strives to consume it.

In consequence of this;

Human society is to conscious existence what unconscious existence in general is to the unconscious individual existence.

I can only develop in and through community with other men. . . . In society, too, the opposition of individual existence and existence in general becomes etc. . . .

Nature . . . is a . . . unity which embraces the infinity of phenomena contained in it.

existence) becomes the soil and the subsistence of its (the individual existence's) development . . . that each is founded upon the other.

That they strive with one another and oppose one another.

It follows:

That conscious individual existence is also conditioned by the conscious totality of existence and *vice versa*. . . .

The individual human being develops only in and through society, society *vice versa*, etc. . . .

Society is a unity which embraces and comprises the infinity of individual human existences.

But our author is not satisfied with this kaleidoscopic display. He goes on to repeat his artless remarks about individuality and totality in yet another form. He first puts forward these arid abstractions as absolute principles and concludes that the same relationship must recur in the real world. This gives him the chance of saying everything twice (his excuse being that he is making deductions), in abstract form and, when he is drawing his conclusion, in seemingly concrete form. Then, however, he sets about juggling with the concrete names which he has given to his two categories. Totality appears variously as nature, unconscious totality of existence, conscious ditto, life in general, world organism, all-embracing unity, human society, community, organic unity of the universe, universal happiness, **common** weal, etc., and individuality appears under the corresponding names of unconscious and conscious individual existence, individual happiness, one's own welfare, etc. The phrases which have already been applied quite often enough to individuality and totality are now applied to each of these names in turn.

The second Cornerstone contains, therefore, nothing which was not already contained in the first. But since the words *égalité, solidarité, unité des intérêts*, are used by the French socialists, our author endeavours to hew them, too, into the semblance of true socialist " Cornerstones." He attempts to Germanize them.

> As a conscious member of society I recognize every other member as a being different from myself, opposed to me and at the same time deriving from the common fundament of our being and equal to me. I recognize every one of my fellow-men as opposed to me by reason of his particular nature yet equal to me by reason of his general nature. The recognition of human equality, of the right of every man to existence, depends therefore upon the consciousness that human nature is common to all; in the same way, love, friendship, justice and all the social virtues are based upon the feeling of natural human affinity and unity. Up to the present, these have been termed obligations and have been imposed upon men; but in a society founded upon the consciousness of man's inward nature, i.e. upon reason and not upon external compulsion, they will become free, natural expressions of life. In a society which conforms to nature, i.e. to reason, the conditions of existence must therefore be equal for all its members, i.e. must be general.

The author displays a marked ability for first of all putting forward an hypothesis in dogmatic fashion and then legitimizing it as a consequence of itself by inserting a " therefore," a " nevertheless," etc. He is equally skilful at smuggling into his peculiar deductions traditional socialistic statements by the use of "if one has," "if it is," "for that reason they must," "in this way it becomes," etc., to help his narrative along.

In the first Cornerstone, the individual and totality, in the guise of society, were opposed to one another. This antithesis now reappears in another form, the individual now being divided within himself into a particular and a general nature. From the general nature of the individual, conclusions are drawn about "human equality" and community. Those conditions of life which are common to men appear as a product of "the essence of man," of nature, whereas they, just as much as the consciousness of equality, are historical products. Not content with this, the author bases his equality "on the original common fundament of existence." We learnt in the prologue that man "is endowed with those general energies and properties which animate all things." We learnt in the first Cornerstone that nature is "the basis of all existence," and so, the "common fundament of being." Our author has, therefore, far outstripped the French. "As a conscious member of society," he has not only demonstrated the equality of men with one another; he has also demonstrated their equality with every flea, every wisp of straw, every stone.

We should be only too pleased to believe that "all the social virtues" of our true socialist are based "upon the feeling of natural human affinity and unity," even though feudal bondage, slavery and the social inequalities of every age have also been based upon this "natural affinity." Incidentally, "natural human affinity" is an historical product which is daily changed at the hands of men; it has always been perfectly natural, however inhuman and contrary to nature it may seem, not only in the judgment of "Man" but also of a later, revolutionary generation.

We learn further, quite by chance, that present society is based upon " external compulsion." By " external compulsion" the true socialists do not understand the restrictive, material conditions of life of given individuals. They see it only as the compulsion exercised by the State in the form of bayonets, police, and cannons, which far from being the foundation of society, are only a consequence of its structure. This question has already been discussed in *The Holy Family*[18] and also in the first volume of this work.

The socialist opposes to present society, which is " based upon external compulsion," the ideal of true society, which is based upon the " consciousness of man's inward nature, i.e. upon reason." It is based, that is, upon the consciousness of consciousness, upon the thought of thought. The true socialist does not differ from the philosophers even in his choice of terms. He forgets that the " inward nature " of men, as well as their " consciousness " of it, " i.e. " their " reason," has at all times been an historical product and that even when, as he believes, the society of men has been based " upon external compulsion," their " inward nature " corresponded to this " external compulsion."

On page 163, individuality and totality follow in the usual procession, in the form of individual and general welfare. You may find similar explanations of their mutual relationship in any handbook of political economy under the heading of competition and also, though better expressed, in Hegel. For example, *Rhenish Annals* :

> By furthering the common welfare, I further my own welfare and by furthering my own welfare, I further the common welfare.

Hegel's *Philosophy of Law* :

> In furthering my own ends, I further the generality of ends, which in turn furthers my ends.[19]

# 114   THE GERMAN IDEOLOGY

Compare also *The Philosophy of Law*, pages 323ff., in which the relation of the citizen to the State is discussed :

> Therefore, as a final consequence, we have the conscious unity of the individual with the general existence, harmony. (*Rhenish Annals*.)
>
> As a final consequence [that is to say] of this polar relationship between the individual and the general existence according to which, on the one hand, the two clash and oppose one another, while on the other, the one is the condition and the basis of the other.

The only " final consequence " of this is the harmony of discord with harmony ; and all that follows from the constant repetition of these familiar phrases is the author's belief that his fruitless wrestling with the categories of individuality and totality is the appropriate form in which social questions should be solved.

Our author concludes with the following flourish :

> Organic society has as its basis universal equality and develops, through the opposition of the individuals to totality, towards unrestricted concord, towards the unity of individual with universal happiness, towards social (!) harmony of society (!!), which is the reflection of universal harmony.

It is false modesty to call this sentence a " cornerstone." It is the Rock of Ages upon which the whole of true socialism is founded.

## Third Cornerstone.

> Man's struggle with nature is based upon the polar opposition of my particular existence to, and its interaction with, universal natural activity. When this struggle appears as conscious activity, it is termed labour.

Surely, on the contrary, the idea of a " polar opposition " is based upon the observation of a struggle between man and nature ? First of all, an abstraction is made from a fact; then it is declared that the fact is based upon the abstraction. That is how to proceed if you want to appear German, profound and speculative.

For example : Fact : The cat eats the mouse.

Reflection: Cat = nature, Mouse = nature ; consumption of mouse by cat=consumption of nature by nature =self-consumption of nature.

Philosophic presentation of the fact : The devouring of the mouse by the cat is based upon the self-consumption of nature.

Having thus obscured man's struggle with nature, the writer goes on to obscure man's conscious activity in relation to nature ; he conceives it as the manifestation of this mere abstraction from the real conflict. The profane word labour is finally smuggled in as the result of this process of mystification. It is a word which our true socialist has had on the tip of his tongue from the start, but which he dared not utter until he had legitimized it in the appropriate way. Labour is constructed from the mere abstract idea of man and nature ; it is thereby defined in a way which is equally appropriate and inappropriate to all stages in the development of labour.

> In consequence, labour is any conscious activity on the part of man whereby he tries to acquire dominion over nature in an intellectual and material sense, so that he may utilize it for the conscious enjoyment of his life and for his intellectual and bodily satisfaction.

We shall only draw attention to the brilliant deduction :

> When this conflict appears as conscious activity, it is termed labour—*therefore* labour is any conscious activity on the part of man," etc.

We owe this profound insight to the " polar opposition."

## THE GERMAN IDEOLOGY

The reader will recall Saint-Simon's statement concerning the free development of all man's capacities, mentioned above, and at the same time remember that Fourier wished to see the present "repellent labour" replaced by "attractive labour." We owe to the "polar opposition" the following philosophic vindication and explanation of these terms:

> But since [the "But" is meant to indicate that there is no connection here] the development, the practical activity, the expression of life *should be* a source of enjoyment and satisfaction, it follows that labour should itself be a development, a maturing of the human capacities and should be a source of enjoyment, satisfaction and happiness. Labour *must*, then, become a free expression of life and so a source of enjoyment.

Here we have what we were promised in the preface to *The Rhenish Annals*; namely, "how far German social science differs in its development up to the present from French and English social science" and what it means "to present the doctrine of communism in a scientific form."

It would be a lengthy and a boring procedure to expose every logical lapse which occurs in the course of these few lines. But let us first consider the offences against formal logic.

To prove that labour, an expression of life, should be a source of enjoyment, it is assumed that life should afford enjoyment in all its expressions. From this the conclusion is drawn that since labour is an expression of life, it too should be a source of enjoyment. Not satisfied with this periphrastic transformation of a postulate into a conclusion, the author proceeds to falsify the conclusion. From the fact that "life should be a source of enjoyment in all its manifestations," he deduces that labour, which is one of these manifestations, "should itself be a maturing and developing of human capacities"; that is to say, a maturing and developing of life once again. It should, in fact, be what it already is. How could labour ever be anything but a "development of human capacities"? But he does not stop there. Because labour should be so, it "must" be so, or still better: because it "should be a maturing and development of human capacities," it must nevertheless become something completely different, namely "a free expression of life," which did not enter into the question at all before this. And whereas the postulate of labour as enjoyment was deduced above from the postulate of the enjoyment of life, the former postulate is now put forward as a consequence of the new postulate of "free expression of life in labour."

As far as the content of the passage is concerned, one cannot quite see why labour has not always been what it ought to be, why it must now become what it ought to be, nor why it should become something which up to now it had no need to be. But of course, one must remember that up to now the essence of man and the polar opposition of man and nature have not been fully explained.

We now have a "scientific vindication" of the communist statement about the common ownership of the products of labour:

> But the product of labour [the recurrent "But" has the same meaning as the previous one] must serve at one and the same time the happiness of the individual, of the labouring individual, and the general happiness. This is effected by reason of the fact that all social activities are complementary and reciprocal.

This statement is merely a copy of what any political economy has to say in praise of competition and the division of labour; of course, the introduction of the word "happiness" weakens the whole idea.

# THE GERMAN IDEOLOGY

Finally, we are given a philosophic vindication of the French organization of labour[20]:

> The view of labour as a free activity offering rich sources of satisfaction, yet at the same time serving the common weal, is the basis of the organization of labour.

One would have expected on the contrary that the organization of labour would be the basis of "labour as a rich source of satisfaction." For, according to our author, labour must first become "a free activity offering rich sources of satisfaction etc.," which implies that this state of affairs has not yet been reached. But for the writer, all that seems to be necessary is to have the concept of labour as free activity.

At the end of the essay the belief is expressed that "results" have been reached.

These "cornerstones" and "results," together with those other granite boulders which are to be found in the *Einundzwanzig Bogen*, the *Bürgerbuch*, and the *Neue Anekdota*, form the rock upon which true socialism *alias* German social philosophy, intends to build its Church.

Let us for a moment listen to a few of the hymns, a few of the fragments of the *cantique allégorique hébraique et mystique* which is chanted in this Church.

## 2. KARL GRUN.

### *The Social Movement in France and Belgium*, or *The Historiography of True Socialism*.

> In sooth, if it were not a matter of discussing the whole horde of them . . . we should probably throw down our pen in disgust. . . . And now, with that same arrogance, it [Mundt's *History of Society*] appears

before its wide circle of readers, before that public which seizes voraciously upon everything displaying the word social because a sure instinct tells it what secrets are hidden in this little word. A writer is doubly to blame, he deserves double reproof, if he sets to work without an inward call!

We shall not reproach Herr Mundt with not knowing anything of the actual achievements of French and English social literature apart from what Herr L. Stein has revealed to him. Stein's book, appearing when it did, was worthy of note. ... But to coin phrases at this stage about Saint-Simon, to call Bazard and Enfantin representatives of the two branches of Saint-Simonism, to follow this up with Fourier and to repeat idle chit-chat about Proudhon, etc. ! ... And yet we would willingly overlook this if he had only portrayed the genesis of social ideas in a new and original way.

This piece of rodomontade forms the introduction to Herr Grün's review of Mundt's *History of Society* (*Neue Anekdota*).

The reader of the review will be amazed at the artistic talent shown in it by Herr Grün; he actually gives, in this guise, a review of his own book, as yet unborn.

We observe in Herr Grün a fusion of true socialism with Young-German literary pretensions—a highly diverting spectacle.[21] The book mentioned above is in the form of letters to a lady—from which the reader may reasonably expect a vision of the profound divinities of true socialism, garlanded with the roses and myrtles of "modern literature." Let us hasten to pluck a few roses:

> The Carmagnole was running through my head ... in any case it is a terrible matter for the Carmagnole to take breakfast in the head of a German writer, even if she does not actually take up permanent quarters there....
>
> If I had old Hegel here, I should box his ears:

What! So nature is the otherness of mind? What! you dullard..!

Brussels is to some extent a reproduction of the Convention; it has its parties of the Mountain and the Valley....

The Lüneburg Heath of politics....

Gay, poetic, inconsequent, fantastic chrysalises....

Restoration liberalism, the cactus without soil, which coiled like a parasite round the seats in the Chamber of Deputies....

That the cactus is neither "soilless," nor a "parasite," and that "gay," "poetic" or "inconsequent" chrysalises do not exist, does not detract from these lovely images.

Amid the deluge [of newspapers and journalists in the Cabinet Montpensier] I feel like a second Noah, despatching his doves to see if he can possibly build a dwelling or plant a vineyard anywhere or come to a reasonable agreement with the infuriated Gods....

No doubt this refers to Herr Grün's activity as a newspaper correspondent.

Camille Desmoulins was a man. The Constituent Assembly was composed of Philistines. Robespierre was a virtuous magnetizer. Modern history, in a word, is a life and death struggle against the grocers and the magnetizers!!!!...

Happiness is a plus, but a plus to the $x$th power....

In fact, happiness $=+^x$, a formula which can only be found in the æsthetic mathematics of Herr Grün.

The organization of labour, what is it? And the peoples replied to the Sphinx with the voice of a thousand newspapers... France sings the strophe, Germany the antistrophe, our old Mystic Germany....

North America is even more distasteful to me than the Old World because its shopkeeping egoism has on its cheeks the bloom of impertinent health.... because everything there is so superficial, so shallowly rooted, I might almost say so provincial. ... You call America the New World; it is the oldest of all Old Worlds; our worn-out clothes are fashionable there. ...

We were only aware that unworn stockings of German manufacture were worn there; but they are of too poor a quality to be "fashionable."

The logically stable security of these institutions. ...
Unless these flowers your heart delight
To be a "man" you have no right!

What wanton grace, what arch innocence! What heroic wrestling with æsthetic problems! This brilliant nonchalance is worthy of a Heine.

We have deceived the reader. Herr Grün's literary graces are not an embellishment of true socialist science, the science is merely the padding between these outbursts of literary gossip, and forms, so to speak, its "social background."

In an essay by Herr Grün, "Feuerbach and the Socialists," the following occurs (*Bürgerbuch*):

To speak of Feuerbach is to speak of all philosophic labours from Bacon of Verulam up to the present; one defines at the same time the ultimate purpose and meaning of philosophy, one sees man as the final result of world history. To do so is a surer, because it is a more profound, method of approach than to bring up wages, competition, the faultiness of constitutions and systems of government. ... We have gained man for ourselves, man who has divested himself of religion, of moribund thoughts, of all that is foreign to him, with all their counterparts in the practical world; we have gained pure, essential Man.

This one sentence is enough to show what kind of "certainty" and "profundity" we have to hope for from Herr Grün. He ignores small questions. Equipped with an unquestioning faith in the conclusions of

German philosophy, as formulated by Feuerbach, viz., that " man," " pure essential man," is the ultimate purpose of world history, that religion is estranged human essence, that human essence is human essence and the measure of all things—believing further in the German socialist truths that money, wage labour, etc., are also an estrangement of human essence, that German socialism is the realization of German philosophy and the theoretical truth of foreign socialism and communism—Herr Grün travels to Brussels and Paris with all the complacency of a true socialist.

The powerful trumpetings of Herr Grün in praise of true socialism and of German science exceed anything his fellow-believers have achieved in this respect. As far as these eulogies refer to true socialism, they are obviously quite sincere. Herr Grün's modesty does not permit him to utter a single sentence that has not already been pronounced by some other true socialist in the *Einundzwanzig Bogen*, the *Bürgerbuch* and the *Neue Anekdota*. Indeed, he devotes his whole book to filling in an outline of the French social movement sketched in the *Einundzwanzig Bogen* by Hess, and to answering a need expressed in the same work on page 88.[22] German philosophy must be deeply indebted to him for his praise of it, seeing how little he knows about it. The national pride of the true socialists, their pride in Germany as the land of " man," of " human essence," as opposed to the other profane nationalities, reaches its climax in him. We give below a few samples of it:

> But I should like to know whether they won't all have to learn from us, these French and English, Belgians and North Americans.

He now enlarges upon this.

> The North Americans appear to me thoroughly prosaic and, despite their legal freedom, it is from us that they will probably have to learn their socialism.

Particularly since they have had, since 1829, their own social democratic school, against which their political economist Cooper was fighting as long ago as 1830.

The Belgian democrats! Do you really think that they are half so far advanced as the Germans? Why, I have just had a tussle with one of them who considered the realization of free humanity to be a chimera!

The nationality of "man," of "human essence," of "humanity" shows off here as vastly superior to Belgian nationality.

Frenchmen! Leave Hegel in peace until you understand him. [We believe that Lerminier's criticism of the philosophy of law, however weak it may be in other respects, shows more insight into Hegel than anything which Herr Grün has written either under his own name or that of "Ernest of the Heath."] Try drinking no coffee, no wine for a year; don't give way to passionate excitement, let Guizot rule and let Algiers come under the sway of Morocco. [How is Algiers ever to come under the rule of Morocco, even if the French were to surrender it?] Sit in a garret and study the Logic and the Phenomenology. And when you come down after a year, lean in frame and red of eye, and go into the street and stumble over some dandy or town crier, don't be abashed. For you will have become in the interval great and mighty men, your mind will be like an oak that is nourished by miraculous (!) sap; whatever you see will yield up to you its most secret weaknesses; though only created spirits, you will penetrate to the heart of nature[23]; your glance will be mortal, your word will move mountains, your dialectic will be keener than the keenest guillotine. You will present yourself at the Hôtel de Ville—and the bourgeoisie is a thing of the past. You will step up to the Palais Bourbon—and it collapses. The whole Chamber of Deputies will disappear into the void. Guizot will vanish, Louis Philippe will fade into an historical ghost and out of all these forces which you have annihilated there will rise victorious the absolute idea of free society. Seriously, you can only subdue Hegel by first of all becoming Hegel yourselves. As I have already remarked—Moor's beloved can only die at the hands of Moor.[24]

The belletristic aroma of these true socialist statements will make everyone sneeze. Herr Grün, like all true socialists, does not forget to bring up again the old chatter about the superficiality of the French:

For I am condemned to find the French mind inadequate and superficial, every time that I come into close contact with it.

Herr Grün does not conceal from us the fact that his book is intended to glorify German socialism as the criticism of French socialism:

The literary riff-raff in Germany call our socialist endeavours an imitation of French perversities. No one has so far considered it worth while to reply anything to this. The riff-raff must surely feel ashamed, if they have any sense of shame at all, when they read this book. They probably never dreamt that German socialism is a criticism of French socialism, that far from considering the French to be the inventors of a new *Contrat Social*, it demands that French socialism should make good its deficiencies by a study of German science. At this moment, an edition of a translation of Feuerbach's *Essence of Christianity* is being prepared here in Paris. May their German schooling do the French much good! Whatever may arise from the economic position of the country or the constellation of present-day politics, only the humanistic outlook will ensure a human existence for the future. The Germans, unpolitical and despised as they are, this people which is no people, will have laid the cornerstone of the building of the future.

## TRUE SOCIALISM

Of course, there is no need for a true socialist, absorbed in his intimacy with " human essence," to know anything about what " may arise from the economic position and the political constellation " of a country.

Herr Grün, as an apostle of true socialism, does not merely, like his fellow-apostles, boast of the omniscience of the Germans as compared with the ignorance of the other nations. Utilizing his experience as a man of letters, he coolly forces himself, like any tourist, into the various socialist, democratic and communist parties and when he has sniffed them from all angles, he presents himself to them as the apostle of true socialism. All that remains for him to do is to teach them, to communicate to them the profoundest discoveries concerning free humanity. The superiority of true socialism over the French parties now assumes the form of the personal superiority of Herr Grün over the representatives of these parties. This gives him a chance not only of utilizing the French party leaders as a pedestal for Herr Grün, but also of talking all sorts of gossip, thereby compensating the German provincial for the exertion which the more pregnant statements of true socialism have caused him.

> Kats pulled a face expressive of plebeian cheerfulness when I assured him of my complete satisfaction with his speech.

Herr Grün lost no time in instructing Kats about French terrorism and

> had the good fortune to win the approval of my new friend.

His effect on Proudhon was different but equally important:

> I had the infinite pleasure of acting, so to speak, as the tutor of the man whose acumen has not perhaps been surpassed since Lessing and Kant.

K

Louis Blanc is merely " his swarthy young friend."

He asked very greedily but also very ignorantly about conditions with us. We Germans know (?) French conditions almost as well as the French themselves; at least we study (?) them.

And we learn of " Papa Cabet " that he " has limitations." Herr Grün set him problems, and Cabet

confessed that he had not exactly been able to fathom them. I [Grün] had long observed this; and that of course meant an end of everything, especially as it occurred to me that Cabet's mission had long ago been fulfilled.

We shall see later how Herr Grün contrives to give Cabet a new " mission."

Let us first deal with the outline and the few wellworn traditional ideas which form the skeleton of Grün's book. Both are copied from Hess, whom Herr Grün paraphrases indeed in the most lordly fashion. Matters which are quite vague and mystical even in Hess, although they were originally—in the *Einundzwanzig Bogen*—worthy of recognition, and have only become tiresome and reactionary as a result of their perpetual reappearance in the *Bürgerbuch*, the *Neue Anekdota* and *The Rhenish Annals*, at a time when they were already out of date, become complete nonsense in Herr Grün's hands.

Hess equates the development of French socialism and German philosophy—Saint-Simon with Schelling, Fourier with Hegel, Proudhon with Feuerbach. Compare, for example, *Einundzwanzig Bogen*, pages 78, 79, 326, 327; *Neue Anekdota*, pages 194, 195, 196, 202 ff. (Parallels between Feuerbach and Proudhon, e.g. Hess: "Feuerbach is the German Proudhon," etc., *Neue Anekdota*, page 202. Grün: "Proudhon is the French Feuerbach," page 404). This schematic exposition provided by Hess is the only thing which gives inner cohesion to Grün's book. But, of course, Herr Grün does not fail to add a few literary flourishes. Even obvious blunders on the part of Hess, e.g. that theoretical constructions form the "social background" and the "theoretical basis" of practical movements (e.g. *Neue Anekdota*, page 192) are copied faithfully by Herr Grün, (e.g. Grün, page 264: "The social background of the political question in the eighteenth century . . . was the simultaneous product of the two philosophic tendencies"—that of the sensualists and that of the deists). He copies, too, the opinion that it is only necessary to put Feuerbach into practice, to apply him to social life, in order to produce the complete critique of existing society. Hess accused French communism and socialism further in the following terms:

> Fourier, Proudhon, etc., did not get beyond the category of wage labour (*Bürgerbuch*, page 40)

and elsewhere:

> Fourier would like to endow the world with new associations of egoism (*Neue Anekdota*, page 196).
> Even the radical French communists are still busy with the opposition of labour and enjoyment. They have not yet grasped the unity of production and consumption (*Bürgerbuch*, page 43).
> Anarchy, the negation of the concept of political rule (*Einundzwanzig Bogen*, page 77 etc.).

If you have read these, you have pocketed the whole of Herr Grün's critique of the French. As a matter of fact he had it in his pocket before he went to Paris. Equipped with these ideas, he finds it fairly easy to settle accounts with the French socialists and communists; he also obtains great assistance from the various traditional phrases current in Germany about religion, politics, nationality, human and inhuman, etc., which have been taken over by the true socialists from the philosophers. All he has to do is to hunt for the words " man " and " human " and condemn when he cannot find them. For example :

You are political ? Then you have your limitations.

In the same way, Herr Grün is enabled to exclaim :

You are national, religious, addicted to political economy, you have a God ? Then you are not human, you have your limitations.

This is a process which he follows throughout his book. He thereby, of course, offers a thorough criticism of politics, nationality, religion, etc., and at the same time clarifies to a remarkable extent the characteristics of the authors criticized and their connection with social development.

One can see from this that Grün's fabrication is on a much lower level than the work by Stein, which at least tried to portray the connection between socialist literature and the real development of French society. It need hardly be mentioned that in the book under discussion, as in the *Neue Anekdota*, Herr Grün adopts the most patronizing manner towards his predecessor.

But has Herr Grün even succeeded in copying correctly what he has taken over from Hess and others ? Has he even incorporated the necessary material in the outline which he took over lock, stock and barrel in the most uncritical fashion ? Has he even given a complete and correct exposition of the individual socialist authors according to the sources ? Surely this is the least one could ask of the man from whom the North Americans, the French, the English and the Belgians have to learn, the man who was the tutor of Proudhon and who perpetually brandishes his German thoroughness before the eyes of the superficial Frenchmen ?

TRUE SOCIALISM 129

(a) *Saint-Simonism.*

Herr Grün has not first-hand knowledge of a single Saint-Simonian book! His main sources are: Firstly, the much despised Ludwig Stein; secondly, Stein's chief source, L. Reybaud (in return for which he proposes to make an example of Herr Reybaud and calls him a Philistine; while on the same page he pretends that he did not come across Reybaud's book until after he had settled with the Saint-Simonists); and occasionally Louis Blanc. We shall give direct proofs.

The main sources for Saint-Simon's life are the fragments of his autobiography in the *Works of Saint-Simon*, published by Olinde Rodrigues, and the *Organisateur* of May 19th, 1830[25] We have, therefore, all the documents here before us: (1) The original sources; (2) Reybaud, who summarized them; (3) Stein, who utilized Reybaud; (4) Herr Grün's literary effusion.

Herr Grün:

> Saint-Simon took part in the American struggle for independence without having any particular interest in the war itself; it had occurred to him that there was a possibility of uniting the two great oceans of the world.

Stein:

> First of all he entered military service . . . and went to America with Bouillé. . . . In this war, the significance of which he, of course, realized . . . " The war, as such," he says, " did not interest me; it was the purpose of this war, etc." . . . After he had vainly tried to interest the Viceroy of Mexico in a grandiose scheme for linking up the two great oceans by canal. . . .

Reybaud:

> A fighter for American independence, he served under Washington. . . . " The war in itself did not

interest me," he said, " but the object of the war interested me keenly and this interest induced me to endure its hardships without demur."

Herr Grün only copies the fact that Saint-Simon himself had " no particular interest in the war "; he omits the whole point—his interest in the object of the war.

Herr Grün further omits to state that Saint-Simon wanted to win the Viceroy's support for his plan and thus gives the impression that the plan was a mere " idea." He likewise omits to mention that Saint-Simon did not do this until the war had ceased, the reason being that Stein indicates this only by giving the date.

Herr Grün proceeds without a break :

> Later [when ?] he plans a Franco-Dutch expedition to the English Indies.

Stein :

> He travelled to Holland in 1785, to plan a joint French and Dutch expedition against the English colonies in India.

Stein is incorrect here and Grün copies him faithfully. According to Saint-Simon, the Duc de la Vauguyon had induced the States General to undertake a joint expedition with France to the English colonies in India. Concerning himself, he merely says that he " worked for the execution of this plan for a year."

Herr Grün :

> When in Spain, he wished to dig a canal from Madrid to the sea.

Saint-Simon wished to dig a canal ? What nonsense ! Previously, it " occurred to him " to do something, now he " wishes " to do something. Grün gets his facts

## TRUE SOCIALISM

wrong this time, not because he copies Stein too faithfully, but because he copies him too superficially.

Stein:

> He returned to France in 1786 but in the very next year he again visited Spain, to present to the Government a plan for the completion of a canal from Madrid to the sea.

Herr Grün, skimming through Stein, receives the impression that the plan of construction and the idea of the whole project originated with Saint-Simon; hence his version. As a matter of fact, Saint-Simon merely drew up a plan to overcome the financial difficulties which beset the building of the canal, which had been begun long since.

Reybaud:

> Six years later, he put before the Spanish Government a plan for the construction of a canal with the object of establishing a navigable route from Madrid to the sea.

The same mistake as that made by Stein.

Saint-Simon, page xvii:

> The Spanish Government had undertaken the construction of a canal which was to link Madrid with the sea; the scheme was in difficulties since the Government lacked labour and funds; M. le Comte de Cabarrus, now Finance Minister, collaborated with me in the following plan, which we presented to the Government, etc.

Herr Grün:

> In France he speculated on national domains.[26]

Stein first of all sketches Saint-Simon's attitude during the revolution and then passes to his speculation in national domains. But where has Herr Grün got the nonsensical expression: " speculated *on* national domains," instead of *in* national domains ? We can best explain it by offering the reader the original :

Reybaud :

> Having returned to Paris, he turned his attention to speculation and dealt in national domains (*trafiqua sur les domaines nationaux*).

Herr Grün does not explain his statement at all. He does not indicate why Saint-Simon should have speculated in national domains and why this fact, trivial in itself, should be of importance in his life. He finds it unnecessary to copy from Stein and Reybaud the fact that Saint-Simon wished to found a scientific school and a great industrial undertaking by way of experiment, and that he intended to raise the necessary capital by these speculations (*Œuvres*, page xix).

Herr Grün :

> He marries so that he may be able to act as the host of science, to investigate the lives of men and exploit them psychologically.

Herr Grün here suddenly skips one of the most important periods of Saint-Simon's life—the period during which he studied natural science and travelled for that purpose. What does marrying to be the host of science mean ? What does marrying in order to exploit men (whom one does not marry) psychologically mean ? The whole point is this : Saint-Simon married so that he could hold a salon and study there among others the men of learning.

Stein puts it in this way :

> He marries in 1801.... " I made use of my married life to study the men of learning." (Cf. Saint-Simon, page xxiii.).

We are now, having seen the original, in a position to understand and explain Herr Grün's nonsense.

## TRUE SOCIALISM

The " psychological exploitation of men " is in Stein and Reybaud merely the observation of men of learning in their social life. It was in conformity with his socialist outlook that Saint-Simon should wish to acquaint himself with the influence of science upon the personality of men of learning and upon their behaviour in ordinary life. For Herr Grün this wish turns into a senseless, vague whim, savouring of the novelette.

Herr Grün :

> He becomes poor [how ?], he becomes a clerk in a pawnshop at a salary of a thousand francs a year—he, a count, a scion of Charlemagne ; then [when and why ?] he lives on the bounty of a former servant of his; then [when and why?] he tries to shoot himself, is rescued and begins a new life of study and propaganda. Only now does he write his two chief works.

" He becomes "—" then "—" later "—" now "—such phrases as these act as substitutes for the links connecting the various periods of Saint-Simon's life.

Stein :

> Then there appeared a new and a fearful enemy—actual poverty, which became more and more oppressive. . . . After a distressing wait of six months . . . he obtained a position—[Herr Grün gets the very dash from Stein but he is cunning enough to insert it after the pawnshop] as clerk in the pawnshop [not, as Herr Grün artfully writes it, " in *a* pawnshop," since it is well known that in Paris there is only one such establishment, and that a public one] at a salary of a thousand francs a year. How his fortune fluctuated in those days ! The grandson of Louis the Fourteenth's famous courtier, the heir to a ducal coronet, to an immense fortune, by birth a peer of France and a Grandee of Spain, a clerk in a pawnshop !

Now we see the source of Herr Grün's pawnshop ; but here, in Stein, the expression is at least appropriate. To accentuate his difference from Stein, Grün only calls

Saint-Simon a " count " and a " scion of Charlemagne."
He has the last fact from Stein and Reybaud, but they
are wise enough to say that Saint-Simon used to trace
his descent from Charlemagne. Stein offers positive
facts which make Saint-Simon's poverty seem surprising
under the Restoration ; but Herr Grün only expresses
his astonishment that a count and an alleged scion of
Charlemagne can possibly find himself in reduced
circumstances.

Stein :

> He lived two more years [after his attempted suicide]
> and perhaps achieved more during them than during
> any two decades earlier in his life. The *Catechism
> of the Industrialists* was completed [Herr Grün trans-
> forms this completion of a work which had long been
> in preparation into : " Not till now did he write," etc.]
> and *The New Christianity*, etc.

On page 169 Stein calls these two books " the two
chief works of his life."

And so Herr Grün has not merely copied the errors
of Stein ; by adapting obscure passages of Stein he has
actually invented new errors. To conceal his plagiarism,
he selects only the outstanding facts ; but he robs them
of their factual character by tearing them out of their
chronological context and omitting, not only the motives
governing them, but even the most vital connecting
links. What we have given above is, literally, all that
Herr Grün has to relate about the life of Saint-Simon.
In his version, the stormy, active life of Saint-Simon
becomes a mere succession of ideas and events which are
of less interest than the life of any peasant or speculator
who lived through those stormy times in one of the
French provinces.

After dashing off this piece of biographical hack-work,
he exclaims : " this full, genuinely civilized life ! " He
does not even shrink from saying : "Saint-Simon's life

is the mirror of Saint-Simonism itself——" as if Grün's life of Saint-Simon were the mirror of anything except Herr Grün's method of patching together a book.

We have spent some time discussing this biography because it is a classical example of the way in which Herr Grün deals *thoroughly* with the French socialists. In this case, to conceal his borrowings, Herr Grün dashes off passages with an air of nonchalance, he omits facts, he falsifies and he transposes; we shall watch him later developing all the symptoms of a plagiarist consumed by inward uneasiness: artificial confusion, to make comparison difficult; omission of sentences and words which he does not quite understand, being ignorant of the original, when quoting his sources; poetical elaboration in the form of phrases of indefinite meaning; treacherous attacks upon the very persons whom he is copying. Herr Grün is indeed so hasty and so precipitous in his plagiarism that he frequently refers to matters which he has never mentioned to his readers but which he, as a reader of Stein, carts round in his own head.

We shall now pass to Grün's exposition of the doctrine of Saint-Simon.

(i) *Letters of an inhabitant of Geneva to his contemporaries.*

Herr Grün did not gather clearly from Stein the connection between the plan for supporting the men of learning, outlined in the work quoted above, and the fantastic appendix to the brochure. He speaks of this work as if it treated mainly of the organization of society and ends as follows:

> The spiritual power in the hands of the men of learning, the temporal power in the hands of the property-owners, the franchise for all. Cf. Stein page 151, Reybaud, page 83.

The sentence :

> The power of nominating the persons called to fill the functions of leaders of humanity should be in the hands of everyone,

which Reybaud quotes from Saint-Simon and which Stein translates in the clumsiest fashion, is reduced by Herr Grün to " the franchise for all," which robs it of all meaning. Saint-Simon is referring to the election of the Newton Council, Herr Grün is referring to elections in general.[27]

Herr Grün dismisses the *Letters* in four or five sentences copied from Stein and Reybaud, but long afterwards, when he has got as far as *The New Christianity*, he suddenly returns to them.

> But it is not to be achieved by abstract knowledge [still less by concrete ignorance, as we observe]. From the standpoint of abstract science, of course, there was still a cleavage between the " property-owners " and " everyone."

Herr Grün forgets that so far he has only mentioned the " franchise for all " and has not mentioned " everyone." But since he finds " everyone " in Stein and Reybaud, he must put " everyone " in inverted commas. He forgets, moreover, that he has not given us the following sentence in Stein, the qualification of the " of course " in his own sentence :

> He [Saint-Simon] makes a distinction apart from the sages or the men of learning, between the property-owners and everyone. It is true that there is no clearly marked boundary between the two latter . . . but nevertheless, there lies in that indefinite idea of "everyone" the germ of that class towards the understanding and uplifting of which his theory was later directed, that most numerous and poorest class, that section of the people which was at that time only potentially present.

Stein stresses the fact that Saint-Simon already makes a distinction between " property-owners " and " everyone," but still a very vague one. Herr Grün twists this so that he appears surprised that Saint-Simon should still make any distinction at all. This is naturally a great mistake on the part of Saint-Simon and is only to be explained by the fact that his standpoint in the *Letters* is that of abstract science. Unfortunately, in the passage in question, Saint-Simon is not speaking about differences in a future order of society, as Herr Grün thinks. He is making an appeal for support to mankind as a whole; as he finds it, it seems to be divided into three classes; not, as Stein believes, into men of learning, owners of property, and everybody; but (1) men of learning and artists and all people of liberal ideas; (2) the opponents of innovation, i.e. the owners of property, in so far as they do not belong to the first class; (3) the surplus of humanity which rallies around the word "equality." These three classes form " everybody." Cf. Saint-Simon, *Lettres*, pages 21, 22. As Saint-Simon also says later that he considers his distribution of power advantageous to all classes, we may take it that in the place where he speaks of this distribution, " everybody " obviously corresponds to the " surplus " which rallies around the word " equality," without, however, excluding the other classes. Stein is roughly correct, although he pays no attention to the passage on pages 21 and 22. Herr Grün, who knows nothing of the original, clutches at Stein's slight error and succeeds in making sheer nonsense of his argument.

We come across an even more striking example almost immediately. We learn unexpectedly on page 94, where Herr Grün is no longer speaking of Saint-Simon but of his school:

In one of his books, Saint-Simon utters the mysterious words: "Women will be admitted, they may even be nominated." From this almost barren seed, the whole gigantic affair of the emancipation of woman has sprung up.

Of course, if in some work or other Saint-Simon did speak of admitting and nominating women, for some unknown purpose, these would indeed be "mysterious words." But the mystery exists only in the mind of Herr Grün. "One of Saint-Simon's books" is none other than the *Letters of an Inhabitant of Geneva*. In this work, after stating that everyone is eligible to subscribe to the Newton Council or its departments, he continues: "Women will be allowed to subscribe, they will be permitted to be nominated"—that is, to a position in this Council or its departments, of course. Stein, as was fitting, quotes this passage in the course of his discussion of the book itself and makes the following comment:

> Here, etc., are to be found the germs of his later opinions and even those of his school; even, too, the first idea of the emancipation of women.

Stein observes quite rightly, in a note, that Olinde Rodrigues printed this passage in large type in his 1832 edition, since it was the only mention of the emancipation of women in Saint-Simon, for polemical reasons. To hide his plagiarisms, Grün shifts the passage from the book to which it belongs to his discussion of the school, makes the above nonsense of it, changes Stein's "germ" into "seed" and childishly pretends that this passage is the origin of the doctrine of the emancipation of women.

Herr Grün ventures an opinion on the contradiction which, he believes, exists between the *Letters* and the *Catechism of the Industrialists*; it consists in the fact that in the *Catechism* the rights of the workers are as-

## TRUE SOCIALISM 139

serted. He knows the *Letters*, of course, only through the medium of Stein and Reybaud, and the *Catechism* similarly. Had he read Saint-Simon himself, he would have found in the *Letters* a " seed " of the point of view developed among others in the *Catechism*. For example:

> All men shall work (*Letters*, page 60).
> If his brain [the rich man's] is not fitted for labour, he will be compelled to work with his hands; for Newton will assuredly not permit on this planet ... workers who, of their own free will, remain idle in the workshops (page 64).

(*ii*) *Political Catechism of the Industrialists.*

As Stein usually quotes this work as the *Catechism of the Industrialists*, Herr Grün knows, of course, of no other title. But since he only devotes ten lines to this work when he comes to speak of it *ex officio*, one might have at least expected him to give it its correct title.

Having copied from Stein the fact that in this work Saint-Simon proposes to put power into the hands of labour, he continues: "He now divides the world into idlers and industrialists."

Herr Grün is wrong here. He credits the *Catechism* with making a distinction which he finds set out much later in Stein, the occasion being a discussion of the school of Saint-Simon:

Stein: "Society consists at present only of idlers and workers." (Enfantin.) Instead of the alleged division, there is in the *Catechism* a division into three classes, the feudal, intermediary and industrial classes; naturally, Herr Grün could not enlarge upon these without recourse to Stein, since he is not familiar with the *Catechism* itself.

Herr Grün then repeats the statement that the content of the *Catechism* is the rule of labour and concludes his account of the work as follows:

## 140  THE GERMAN IDEOLOGY

Just as republicanism proclaims: Everything for the people, everything through the people, Saint-Simon proclaims: Everything for industry, everything through industry.

Stein:

Since industry is the source of everything, everything must serve industry.

Stein rightly notes that, as early as 1817, a work of Saint-Simon's, *Industry*, bears the motto: All through industry, all for industry. In the course of his account of the *Catechism*, Herr Grün therefore not only commits the error mentioned above but also misquotes the motto of a much earlier work of which he has no knowledge whatever.

According to the standards of German thoroughness, this constitutes an adequate criticism of the *Political Catechism of the Industrialists*. But we find scattered throughout Grün's omnium gatherum isolated glosses which belong properly to this section. Chuckling over his own slyness, Herr Grün distributes the material which he finds in Stein's review of the work and elaborates it with commendable courage.

Herr Grün:

Free competition was an impure and confused notion, a notion which contained in itself a new world of conflict and misery, the struggle between capital and labour and the misery of the worker deprived of capital. Saint-Simon purified the concept industry; he reduced it to the idea of labour, he formulated the rights and grievances of the fourth estate, of the proletariat. He was forced to abolish the right of inheritance, since it had become an injustice towards the worker, towards the industrialist. This is the significance of his *Catechism of the Industrialists*.

Herr Grün found that when dealing with the *Catechism*, Stein observed:

Here therefore we have the true significance of Saint-Simon; he foresaw that this opposition (of bourgeoisie and people) was a precise one.

This is the source of Herr Grün's idea of the " significance " of the *Catechism*.

Stein :

> He [Saint-Simon in the *Catechism*] begins with the concept of the industrial worker.

Herr Grün makes complete nonsense of this; he asserts that Saint-Simon, who found free competition an " impure idea," purified " the idea of industry " and reduced it to the " idea of labour." It is clear that Herr Grün's idea of industry and free competition is a very " impure " and a very " confused " one indeed.

Herr Grün goes from strength to strength; he risks a direct falsehood and states that Saint-Simon desired to abolish the right of inheritance.

On page 88 he tells us, still relying on his interpretation of Stein's version of the *Catechism* :

> Saint-Simon established the rights of the proletariat. He uttered the new watchword : the industrialists, the workers, shall be raised to a position of supreme power. This was one-sided, but every struggle involves onesidedness; he who is not one-sided cannot wage a conflict.

Despite his eloquent maxims about one-sidedness, Herr Grün commits the one-sided error of understanding Stein to say that Saint-Simon wished to " raise " the actual workers, the proletarians, " on to the ladder leading to power." Cf. page 102, where he says of Michel Chevalier :

> M. Chevalier still refers with great sympathy to the industrialists. . . . But to the disciple, the industrialists are no longer, as they were for his master, the proletarians; he includes capitalists, entrepreneurs

L

and workers in one concept, that is to say, he includes the idlers in a category which should only embrace the poorest and most numerous class.

Saint-Simon numbers among the industrialists not only the workers but also the manufacturers, the merchants, in short, all industrial capitalists; indeed, he addresses himself primarily to them. Herr Grün could have found this on the very first page of the *Catechism*. But one can see how, without ever having seen the work, he concocts from hearsay fine phrases about it.

Discussing the *Catechism*, Stein says:

> After, etc. . . Saint-Simon comes to a history of industry in its relation to state authority . . . he is the first to be conscious that in the science of industry there lie hidden political factors . . . It is undeniable that he made a real discovery. Before him, France did not possess a history of political economy.

Stein himself is extremely vague when he speaks of "political factors" or "science of industry." But he shows that he is on the right track by adding that the history of the State is intimately connected with the history of national economy.

Let us see how Herr Grün, in his discussion of the school of Saint-Simon, appropriates these fragments of Stein:

> Saint-Simon had attempted a history of industry in his *Catechism of the Industrialists*, stressing the political element in it. The master himself opened the way, therefore, to political economy.

Herr Grün "therefore" transforms the "political factor" of Stein into a "political element" and makes it meaningless by omitting the details given by Stein. This "stone which the builders have rejected" has indeed become for Herr Grün the "cornerstone" of his "letters and studies." But it has also become for him a stumbling-block. Let us proceed. Whereas Stein says that Saint-Simon paved the way for a history of political economy by stressing the political factor in the science of industry, Herr Grün makes him himself the pioneer of political economy. Herr Grün argues something after this fashion: Economic science was already known of before Saint-Simon; but as Stein relates, he stressed the political factor in industry, therefore he made economics political—political economics=political economy—and so Saint-Simon opened the way to political economy. Herr Grün's conjectures undoubtedly display great serenity of mind.

Just as he makes Saint-Simon the pioneer of political economy, he makes him the pioneer of scientific socialism:

> It [Saint-Simonism] contains ... scientific socialism, for Saint-Simon spent his whole life searching for the new science!

(iii) *The New Christianity.*

With his customary brilliance, Herr Grün gives us ornate extracts of extracts by Stein and Reybaud, which he dismembers in the most pitiless fashion. One example will suffice to show that he has never looked at the original of this work either.

> Saint-Simon aimed at establishing a unified outlook, such as is suitable to organic periods of history, which he expressly opposes to the critical periods. According to him, we have been living since Luther in a critical period: he thought to initiate a new organic period. Hence *The New Christianity.*

At no time and in no place did Saint-Simon ever oppose organic to critical periods of history. This is an actual falsehood on the part of Herr Grün. Bazard was the first to make this distinction. Herr Grün discovered from Stein and Reybaud that in *The New Christianity* Saint-Simon commends the criticism of Luther, but finds his positive, dogmatic doctrine faulty. Herr Grün merges this with what he remembers was said in the same sources about the school of Saint-Simon, and fabricates out of the two the above assertion.

After some florid comments on Saint-Simon's life and works, for which his only authorities are Stein and the latter's guiding star, Reybaud, he concludes by exclaiming:

> And those moral Philistines, Herr Reybaud and the whole mob of gossiping German parrots, thought that they had to make apologies for Saint-Simon, by pronouncing with their usual wisdom that such a man, such a life, must not be measured by ordinary standards! Tell me, are your standards made of wood? Tell the truth! We shall be quite pleased if they are made of good solid oak. Hand them over! We shall accept them as a precious gift. We shall not burn them, God forbid! We shall use them to belabour the backs of the Philistines.

It is by affected bluster of this kind that Herr Grün attempts to prove his superiority over the men whom he has copied.

### (iv) *The School of Saint-Simon.*

Herr Grün has read just as much of the school of Saint-Simon as he read of Saint-Simon himself— nothing whatsoever. That being so, he should at least have made a proper summary of Stein and Reybaud, he should have observed the chronological order, he should have given a connected account of the course of the events and he should have mentioned the essential points. He does the contrary. Led astray by his bad conscience, he mixes everything up as far as possible, omits the most essential matters, and produces a confusion even greater than that which we saw in his exposition of Saint-Simon. We must be more concise here, however. It would take a volume as thick as Herr Grün's to record every plagiarism and every blunder.

We are given no information about the period from the death of Saint-Simon to the July Revolution—a period which covers part of the most important theoretical development of Saint-Simonism. And so the Saint-Simonian criticism of existing conditions, the most important aspect of Saint-Simonism, simply does not exist for Herr Grün. It would, of course, have been hard for him to say anything about it without a knowledge of the sources, namely the newspapers.

Herr Grün opens his survey of the Saint-Simonists with these words:

> To each according to his capacity, to each capacity according to its works: that is the practical dogma of the Saint-Simonists.

Herr Grün, like Reybaud, presents this sentence as a transition from Saint-Simon to the Saint-Simonists; Herr Grün continues:

> It derives directly from the last words of Saint-Simon: "All men must be assured the freest development of their faculties."

Herr Grün wished to phrase his version differently from Reybaud, who links the "practical dogma" with *The New Christianity*. He believes this to be an invention of Reybaud's and substitutes the last words of Saint-Simon for the *New Christianity*. He did not realize that Reybaud was only giving a literal extract from the *Doctrine de Saint-Simon, Exposition, première année*, page 70. Herr Grün cannot understand why Reybaud, after giving several extracts concerning the religious hierarchy of Saint-Simonism, should suddenly introduce the "practical dogma." Herr Grün imagines that the hierarchy follows directly from this statement; but in fact, the statement can only apply to a new hierarchy when taken in conjunction with the religious ideas of *The New Christianity*. (Apart from these ideas, it can demand at most a purely secular classification of society.) He observes on page 91 :

> To each according to his capacity means to make the Catholic hierarchy the law of the social order. To each capacity according to its works means to turn the workshop into a sacristy and the whole of civil life into a priestly preserve.

The situation is this : Reybaud stated in the extract from the *Exposition* mentioned above :

> The truly universal Church shall appear . . . the universal Church shall govern temporally as well as spiritually . . . science shall be holy, industry shall be holy . . . and all property shall be the property of the Church, every profession a religious function, a step in the social hierarchy. To each according to his capacity, to each capacity according to its works.

To produce his own quite incomprehensible sentence, Herr Grün had only to invert this sentence and change the preceding sentences into conclusions of the final sentence.

Grün's interpretation of Saint-Simonism assumes " so confused and tangled a form " that on page 90 he first makes the " practical dogma " give rise to a " spiritual proletariat," then from the spiritual proletariat he produces a " hierarchy of minds." Finally, out of the hierarchy of minds he produces the apex of the hierarchy. Had he read the *Exposition*, he would have seen how the religious approach of *The New Christianity*, together with the problem of how to determine "capacity," necessitates the hierarchy and its apex.

Herr Grün concludes his discussion and criticism of the *Exposition* of 1828–9 with the single sentence :

To each according to his capacity, to each capacity according to its works.

He hardly even mentions the *Producteur* and the *Organisateur*.[28] He glances at Reybaud and finds in the section : Third Epoch of Saint-Simonism, page 126 (Stein, page 205) :

... and during the following days *The Globe*[29] appeared with the sub-title : *Journal of the Saint-Simonian Doctrine*, which was summarized as follows on the first page :

Religion.

Science.       Industry.

Universal Association.

Herr Grün passes from the above to the year **1831**, without a break, and improves upon Reybaud in the following terms :

The Saint-Simonists put forward the following skeleton of their system ; the formulation was largely the work of Bazard :

Religion.

Science.       Industry.

Universal Association.

Herr Grün leaves out three sentences which are also to be found on the title-page of *The Globe*, and which all relate to practical reforms. They are given by Stein and Reybaud. This enables him to change what is, so to speak, the mere window-dressing of the paper into a " skeleton " for a system. He suppresses the fact that the skeleton appeared on the title-page of *The Globe* and so can criticize the whole of Saint-Simonism, as contained in the mutilated title of a newspaper, with the clever comment that religion has pride of place. He could have discovered from Stein that this is not true of *The Globe*. *The Globe* contains a most detailed

148            THE GERMAN IDEOLOGY

and valuable criticism of existing conditions and particularly of economic conditions—a fact which Herr Grün could not be expected to know. Where can Herr Grün have obtained the important news that the " formulation of the skeleton," four words in length, was " largely the work of Bazard ?"

Herr Grün now jumps from January 1831 back to October 1830.

> Shortly after the July Revolution, during the Bazard period, the Saint-Simonists addressed a short but comprehensive statement of their beliefs to the Chamber of Deputies, after Messrs. Dupin and Mauguin had accused them from the tribune of preaching community of goods and wives.

The address follows, with the comment by Herr Grün :

> How reasonable and measured it all is still ! Bazard was responsible for the form in which it was presented to the Chamber.

We may note, with reference to this concluding remark, that Stein says :

> Judging from its form and its attitude, we should not hesitate to ascribe it [the document], as does Reybaud, to Bazard more than to Enfantin.

And that Reybaud says :

> Judging from the form and the very moderate demands of this document, it is easy to see that the influence of M. Bazard upon its composition was stronger than that of his colleague.

With characteristic ingenuity and intrepidity, Grün turns Reybaud's conjecture that Bazard rather than Enfantin was behind the Address, into the certainty that he drew it up in its entirety. He introduces his reference to the Address with almost the same words as Reybaud :

## TRUE SOCIALISM

Messrs. Dupin and Mauguin drew attention from the tribune to a sect which was preaching community of goods and community of wives.

Strict chronology cannot be reconciled with Herr Grün's method of emancipating himself from those who have trodden the ground before him ; and so he leaves out the date given by Reybaud and contents himself with : " shortly after the July Revolution." Other deviations from Stein are that he inserts in the text what Stein relegates to a note, he omits the introduction to the Address, he translates *fonds de production* (productive capital) simply as " property " and *classement social des individus* (social classification of persons) as " social organization of individuals."

Some lascivious notes follow on the history of the school of Saint-Simon ; they have been patched together from fragments of Stein, Reybaud and Louis Blanc with that artistic skill which we noticed in Grün's life of Saint-Simon. The reader can look them up in the book for himself.

The reader now has before him all that Herr Grün has to say of the Bazard period of Saint-Simonism, i.e. the period from the death of Saint-Simon to the first schism. Grün is now in a position to play an elegantly critical trump, and call Bazard a " poor dialectician." He continues :

> But so are the republicans. They only know how to die, Cato as much as Bazard ; if they do not stab themselves to death, they die of a broken heart.
> A few months after this quarrel, his (Bazard's) heart was broken (Stein).

Such republicans as Levasseur, Carnot, Barrère, Billaud-Varennes, Buonarotti, Teste, D'Argenson, etc., etc., bear out Herr Grün's assertion.

We are now offered a few commonplaces about

Enfantin. Attention need only be drawn to the following discovery:

> Does this historical phenomenon not make it clear that religion is nothing but sensualism, that materialism can boldly claim the same origin as the sacred dogmas themselves?

Herr Grün looks complacently about him:

> Has anyone else ever thought of that?

He would never have "thought of that" if *The Halle Annals*[30] had not already "thought of it" with reference to the romantics. One would have expected Herr Grün to have made some little intellectual progress since then.

He knows, as we have seen, nothing of the whole economic criticism of the Saint-Simonists. Nevertheless, he manages to say something, with the help of Enfantin, about the economic consequences of Saint-Simonism, to which he has already made some airy references. He finds in Reybaud and in Stein extracts from Enfantin's political economy but here, too, he falsifies the original. The abolition of taxes on the most necessary commodities is correctly shown by Reybaud and Stein (who base their statements on Enfantin) to be a consequence of the proposals concerning the right of inheritance; Grün makes it an insignificant, independent measure, over and above these proposals. He gives additional proof of his orginality by falsifying the chronological order; he refers first to the priests Enfantin and Menilmontant and then to Enfantin the economist, whereas his predecessors deal with Enfantin's economic theory during the Bazard period when they are discussing *The Globe*, for which it was written. He merges the Bazard period with the Menilmontant period and later, when referring to economics and to M. Chevalier, he again brings in the Menilmontant period. The occasion for this is the

*Livre nouveau* and as usual he turns Reybaud's conjecture that M. Chevalier was the author of this work into a categorical assertion.

Herr Grün has now presented us with Saint-Simonism in its "totality." He has kept the promise he made "not to subject this literature to a critical scrutiny" and has instead got mixed up, most uncritically, in quite a different "literature," that of Stein and Reybaud. He gives us by way of compensation a few facts about M. Chevalier's economic lectures of 1841–2, by which time he had long ceased to be a Saint-Simonist. While writing about Saint-Simonism, Herr Grün had in front of him a review of these lectures in the *Revue des deux mondes*. He has made use of it in the same way as he utilized Stein and Reybaud. Here is a sample of his critical acumen:

> In it he asserts that not enough is being produced. That is a statement worthy of the old economic school with its rusty prejudices . . . As long as political economy ignores the fact that production is dependent upon consumption, this so-called science will not throw up any shoots.

One can see what a sovereign advantage Herr Grün has over any economic work, with these phrases about consumption and production which he has inherited from true socialism. Apart altogether from the fact that any economist would tell him that supply depends on demand, i.e. that production depends on consumption, there is actually in France a special economic school, that of Sismondi, which desires to make production dependent on consumption in a form different from that which obtains under free competition; it stands in sharp opposition to the economists attacked by Herr Grün. Not till later, however, do we see Herr Grün speculating successfully with the talent entrusted to him—the unity of production and consumption.

The reader deserves some compensation for the boredom he has suffered from these sketchy, falsified, adulterated and diffuse extracts from Stein and Reybaud. And so he is treated to the following Young-German firework display, glowing with humanism and socialism:

> As a social system, Saint-Simonism was nothing more than a cascade of thoughts, showered with beneficent effect upon the soil of France [earlier, it was described as " a flood of light, but a chaos of light "! " not yet an ordered clarity "!!]. It was an overwhelming and yet an amusing display. The author died before the show was put on, one producer died during the performance, the remaining producers and all the actors discarded their costumes, slipped into their civilian clothes, went home, and behaved as if nothing had happened. It was a spectacle, an interesting spectacle, if somewhat confused towards the finale; a few of the actors made a gallant sortie—and that was the end of it all.

How just was Heine's reproof to his imitators: "I sowed dragon's teeth and there has sprung up a race of fleas."[31]

### (b) *Fourierism.*

Apart from the translation of a few passages from the *Four Movements* on the subject of love, there is nothing here that cannot be found in a more complete form in Stein. Herr Grün dismisses morality in a sentence which a hundred other writers had uttered long before Fourier:

> Morality is, according to Fourier, nothing but the systematic endeavour to repress the human passions.

That is how Christian morality has always defined itself. Herr Grün makes no attempt to investigate Fourier's criticism of present-day agriculture and industry and, as far as trade is concerned, he merely translates a few general remarks from the introduction to a section of

*The Four Movements* (*Origin of Political Economy and of the Mercantile Controversy*, pages 332, 334 of *The Four Movements*). Then come a few extracts from *The Four Movements* and one on the French Revolution from *The Treatise on Association*, together with *The Tables on Civilization* which are already known from Stein. The critical side of Fourier, his most important work, is thus dismissed in the most hasty and superficial fashion in twenty-eight pages of literal translation; and in these, with very few exceptions, only the most general and abstract matters are discussed, the trivial and the important being thrown together in the most haphazard way.

Herr Grün now gives us an exposition of Fourier's system. Chouroa, whose work is quoted by Stein, long ago gave us a better and more complete version. Herr Grün considers it vitally necessary, of course, to offer a profound interpretation of Fourier's series; he can, however, think of nothing better than to quote literally from Fourier himself and, as we shall see later, to coin a few fine phrases about numbers. He never thinks of showing how Fourier came to deal with series, and how he and his disciples constructed them; he reveals nothing whatever about the inner construction of these series. Unless one demonstrates how such constructions can be made, one has not proved oneself master of them and no criticism, in the real sense of the word, has been offered, which is true also of criticisms of the Hegelian method. Lastly, Herr Grün neglects almost entirely a matter to which Stein gives at any rate some attention, the opposition of " repellent labour " and " attractive labour."

The most important aspect of the whole exposition is Herr Grün's criticism of Fourier. The reader may recollect what was said above concerning the sources of Grün's criticism. He will now see from the few examples which follow how Herr Grün first of all accepts the postulates of true socialism and then sets about exaggerating and distorting them. It need hardly be mentioned that Fourier's distinction between capital, talent and labour offers a magnificent opportunity for a display of pretentious cleverness; one can spread oneself on the impracticability and the injustice of the distinction, on the introduction of wage labour, without criticizing it by reference to the real relationship of labour and capital. Proudhon has already said all this infinitely better than Herr Grün, but even he failed to touch upon the real issue.

Herr Grün bases his criticism of Fourier's psychology on " the essence of man," the basis, indeed, of all his criticism :

> For human essence is all in all. . . .
> Fourier, too, appeals to this human essence and reveals to us its inward dwelling (!) in his tabulation of the twelve passions ; like every honest and reasonable being, he too desires to make man's inner being a reality, a practical reality. That which is latent must be made patent, so that the distinction between the external and the internal may be utterly destroyed. The history of mankind teems with socialists, if this is to be their distinguishing feature. . . . The important thing about everyone is what he understands by the essence of man.

Or rather the important thing for the true socialists is to foist upon everyone thoughts about human essence and to transform the different stages of socialism into different philosophies of human essence. This unhistorical abstraction induces Herr Grün to proclaim the abolition of all distinction between the internal and the external man, which would even put a stop to the propagation of human essence. But in any case, why should the Germans brag so loudly of their knowledge of human essence ? It does not go beyond the knowledge of the three general attributes, intellect, emotion and will, which have been fairly universally recognized since the days of Aristotle and the Stoics. Herr Grün is also induced to reproach Fourier with having " cleft " man into twelve passions :

> I shall not discuss the completeness of this table, psychologically speaking ; I consider it inadequate—[whereupon the public can rest easy, " psychologically speaking "]—Does this number give us any knowledge of what man really is ? Not for a moment. Fourier might just as well have enumerated the five senses ; the whole man is seen to be contained in these, if they be properly explained and their human content rightly interpreted [as if this " human content " is not entirely dependent on the stage of development which production and human intercourse have reached.] Yes, it is in one sense alone that the essential man is contained, in feeling ; man does not feel as do animals, etc.

For the first time in his whole book, Herr Grün is obviously making an effort to say something about Fourier's psychology from the standpoint of Feuerbach. It is obvious too that this " whole man," " contained " in a single attribute of a real individual and interpreted by the philosopher in terms of that attribute, is a complete chimera. Man must be viewed in his real historical activity and existence. What manner of man can possibly be deduced from the lobe of his own ear, or from some other feature which distinguishes him from the beasts ? Such a man is contained in himself, like his own pimple. Of course, the discovery that human feeling is human and not animal not only makes all psychological experiment superfluous but also constitutes a critique of all psychology.

Herr Grün finds it an easy matter to criticize Fourier's treatment of love ; he measures Fourier's criticism of existing erotic relationships against the fantasies by which Fourier tried to give himself a picture of free love. Herr Grün takes these as seriously as any German Philistine. Indeed, they are the only thing which he does take seriously. It is hard to see why, if he wanted to deal with this side of the system at all, Grün did not enlarge upon Fourier's remarks concerning education; they are the best of their kind and contain some masterly observations. Herr Grün, typical Young-German man of letters that he is, betrays, when he treats of love, how little he has learnt from Fourier's critique. In his opinion, it is of no consequence whether one proceeds from the abolition of marriage or from the abolition of private property; the one must necessarily follow upon the other. But to wish to proceed from any dissolution of marriage other than that which now exists in practice in civil society, is to cherish a purely literary illusion. This very Fourier, as Grün might have discovered, always proceeds from the transformation of production.

Herr Grün is surprised that Fourier, who always starts with inclination (or rather attraction), should indulge in all kinds of " mathematical " experiments, for which reason he calls him the " mathematical socialist." He makes no attempt, of course, to take Fourier's circumstances into account; but he might well have examined a little more closely the nature of attraction. He would very soon have discovered that a natural relation of the kind cannot be accurately defined without the help of calculation. He regales us instead with a literary philippic against number, in which he finds inspiration in the Hegelian tradition. It contains passages such as:

> Fourier takes your most abnormal taste and calculates its molecular content,

indeed, a miracle; and further:

> That civilization, which is being so bitterly attacked,

is based upon an unfeeling multiplication table. . . . Number is not definite. . . . What is the number One ? . . . The number One is restless, it becomes Two, Three, Four [like the German country parson who is "restless" until he has a wife and nine children. . . .] Number stifles all that is essential and all that is real ; can we halve reason or speak of the third of a truth ? [he might also have asked, can we speak of a green-coloured logarithm ?] Number loses all relevance in organic development [a statement of fundamental importance for physiology and organic chemistry]. He who makes number the measure of all things becomes, nay, is an egoist.

By a piece of wilful exaggeration, he links to this sentence another, which he has taken over from Hess (*see above*) :

> Fourier's whole plan of organization is based upon egoism and nothing but egoism. . . . Fourier is the very worst expression of civilized egoism.

He supplies immediate proof of this by relating how, in Fourier's world order, the poorest member eats from forty dishes, how five meals are eaten daily, how people live to the age of 144 and so on. Fourier opposes a Gargantuan view of man to the unassuming mediocrity of the Restoration period ; but Herr Grün only sees in this a chance of moralizing in his Philistine way upon the most innocent side of Fourier's fancy, which he abstracts from the rest.

In the course of reproaching Fourier for his interpretation of the French Revolution, Herr Grün gives us a glimpse of his own insight into the revolutionary age:

> If association had only been known of forty years earlier [so he makes Fourier say], the Revolution could have been avoided. But how [asks Herr Grün] did it come about that Turgot recognized the right to work and that, in spite of this, Louis the Sixteenth lost his head ? After all, it would have been easier

**M**

## THE GERMAN IDEOLOGY

to discharge the national debt by means of the right to work than by means of hen eggs.

Herr Grün overlooks the trifling fact that the right to work, which Turgot speaks of, is none other than free competition and that this very free competition needed the Revolution in order to establish itself.

The substance of Herr Grün's criticism of Fourier is that he failed to subject " civilization " to a " fundamental criticism." And why did he fail ? Here is the reason :

> Its appearance has been criticized and not its bases ; it has been subjected to loathing and ridicule as it exists, but its roots have not been examined. Neither politics nor religion have undergone a searching criticism and for that reason the essence of man still remains to be investigated.

So Herr Grün declares the real circumstances of men to be appearance, whereas religion and politics are the foundation and the root of this appearance. This insipid statement shows how the true socialists proclaim the ideological phrases of German philosophy to be truths higher than the real descriptions and arguments of the French socialists ; it shows at the same time how they try to link the results of French social criticism to the true object of their own investigations, human essence. If one assumes religion and politics to be the basis of material living conditions, then it is only natural that everything should amount in the last instance to an investigation of human essence, i.e. of man's consciousness of himself. One can see, incidentally, how little Herr Grün minds what he copies ; in a later passage and in *The Rhenish Annals* as well, he appropriates what *The Franco-German Annals* had to say about the relation of citizen and bourgeois, which directly contradicts the statement he makes above.[32]

## TRUE SOCIALISM

True socialism confided to Herr Grün's keeping a statement concerning production and consumption. We have reserved his exposition of this to the end. It is a striking example of how Herr Grün measures the postulates of true socialism against the achievements of the French and how, by tearing the former out of their vague obscurity, he reveals them to be utter nonsense.

Production and consumption can be separated temporally and spatially, in theory and in external reality, but in essence they are one. Does not the commonest occupation, e.g. the baking of bread, involve productive activity, which is in its turn consumption for a hundred others? Is it not, indeed, consumption on the part of the baker himself, who consumes corn, water, milk, eggs, etc.? Is not the consumption of shoes and clothes production in relation to cobblers and tailors? Do I not produce when I eat bread? I produce on an enormous scale. I produce mills, kneading-troughs, ovens and as a result, ploughs, harrows, flails, mill-wheels, the labour of woodworkers and masons [and " as a result," carpenters, masons and peasants, " as a result," their parents, " as a result," their whole ancestry, " as a result," Adam]. Do I not consume when I produce? On a huge scale, too. ... If I read a book, I consume first of all the product of whole years of work ; if I keep it or destroy it, I consume the material and the activity of the paper-mill, the printing-press and the book-binder. But do I produce nothing ? I produce perhaps a new book and thereby new paper, new type, new printer's ink, new book-binding tools ; if I merely read it and a thousand others read it too, we produce by our consumption a new edition and all the materials necessary for its manufacture. The manufacturers of all these consume on their part a mass of raw material which must be produced and which can only be produced through the medium of consumption. ... In a word, activity and enjoyment are one, only a perverted world has torn them asunder and has

## 160    THE GERMAN IDEOLOGY

thrust between them the idea of value and price; by so doing, it has torn man asunder and with man, society.

Production and consumption are, in reality, frequently opposed to one another. But in order to restore the unity of the two and resolve all contradictions, one need only interpret these contradictions correctly and comprehend the true nature of production and consumption. This German-ideological theory fits the existing world perfectly, of course; the unity of production and consumption is proved by means of examples drawn from present-day society, it exists in itself. All that Herr Grün succeeds in proving is that there actually does exist a relationship between production and consumption. He argues that he cannot wear a coat or eat bread unless both are produced and unless there exist in society people who produce coats, shoes and bread which other people consume. This idea is, in Herr Grün's opinion, a new one. He clothes it in his classical, literary-ideological language. For example :

> It is believed that the enjoyment of coffee, sugar, etc. is mere consumption; but is this enjoyment not, in fact, production in the colonies ?

He might just as well have asked : Does not this enjoyment imply that negro slaves enjoy the lash and that whips are produced in the colonies ? One can see how such exuberance as this merely serves to conceal an apology for existing conditions. Herr Grün's second idea is that when he produces, he consumes raw material, the costs of production in fact; this is the discovery that nothing produces nothing, that he must start with material. He would have found set out in any political economy, under the heading "reproductive consumption," the complications which this involves; but of course, such difficulties do not arise if one restricts oneself, like

Herr Grün, to the trivial fact that shoes cannot be made without leather.

So far, Herr Grün has convinced himself that you must produce in order to consume and that raw material is consumed in the productive process. His real difficulties begin when he wishes to prove that he produces when he consumes. Herr Grün makes an attempt to enlighten himself in some small degree upon the most commonplace aspect of supply and demand. He is completely unsuccessful. He does discover that his consumption, i.e. his demand, produces a fresh supply. But he forgets that his demand must be effective, that he must offer an equivalent for the product desired, if his demand is to cause fresh production. The economists refer in similar terms to the inseparability of consumption and production and to the absolute identity of supply and demand, when they wish to prove that over-production never takes place; but they never perpetrate anything so clumsy, so trivial as Herr Grün. It is indeed by sophistry of this sort that the aristocracy, the clergy and the rentiers, etc., have always proved their own productivity. Herr Grün forgets, further, that the bread which is produced to-day by steam mills, was produced earlier by wind-mills and water-mills and earlier still by hand-mills; he forgets that these different methods of production are quite independent of the actual eating of the bread and that we are faced, therefore, with an historical development of the productive process. Of course, producing as he does on " an enormous scale," Herr Grün never thinks of this.

He has no inkling of the fact that these different stages of production involve different relations of production to consumption, different contradictions of the two; it does not occur to him that the particular mode of production, together with the whole set of social conditions based upon it, must be taken into account if we are to understand these contradictions ; that they must be changed practically if we are to solve these contradictions. Judged by his other examples, Herr Grün surpasses even the most undistinguished economists in banality ; the example of the book shows him to be far less " humane " than they. They, at least, do not demand that as soon as he has consumed a book he should produce another. They are content that he should produce his own education by his consumption and so exert a favourable influence upon production in general. Herr Grün's reproductive consumption has something miraculous about it. The reason is that he has omitted the connecting link, the cash payment ; he makes it superfluous by merely ignoring it, but in fact it alone makes his demand effective. He reads, and by the mere fact of his reading, he enables the type-founders, the paper merchants and the printers to produce new type, new paper, and new books. The mere fact of his consumption compensates them all for their costs of production. We have already done justice to the virtuosity with which Herr Grün produces new books from old by merely reading the latter, and with which he incurs the gratitude of the whole commercial world by his activities as a producer of new paper, new type, new printer's ink and new book-binding tools. Grün ends the first letter in his book with the words : " I am on the point of plunging into industry." Herr Grün, throughout the whole of his work, never once belies this motto of his.

What did all his activity amount to ? In order to prove the true socialist proposition of the unity of production and consumption, Herr Grün takes refuge in the most commonplace economic statements concerning supply and demand ; moreover, he adapts these to his purpose simply by omitting the necessary connecting links, thereby transforming them into pure fantasies.

He has, in short, carried out an ill-informed and fantastic transfiguration of existing conditions.

In his socialistic conclusion, he lisps, characteristically, the phrases he has learnt from his German predecessors. Production and consumption are separated because a perverse world has torn them asunder. How did a perverse world set about it ? It thrust a concept between the two. By so doing, it tore man asunder. Not content with this, it tears society, i.e. itself, asunder, too. This tragedy took place in 1845.

The true socialists originally understood the unity of production and consumption to mean that activity shall itself involve enjoyment (for them, of course, a purely imaginary notion). Herr Grün gives a further definition of it: "Consumption and production, economically speaking, must coincide." There must be no surplus of products over and above the immediate needs of consumption, which means, of course, the end of any movement whatsoever. With a great show of importance, he actually reproaches Fourier with wishing to disturb this unity by over-production. Herr Grün forgets that over-production causes crises only through its influence on the exchange-value of products and that neither Fourier nor he himself, in his own perfect world, gives a place to exchange-value. All that one can say of this Philistine rubbish is that it is worthy of true socialism.

Herr Grün returns again and again, with the utmost complacency, to his commentary on the true socialist theory of production and consumption. For example, he tells us in the course of a discussion of Proudhon :

> Preach the social freedom of the consumer and you will have true equality of production.
>
> That is an easy matter ! All that has hitherto been wrong has been that " consumers have been uneducated, uncultured, they do not all consume in a human way."

## 164 THE GERMAN IDEOLOGY

The view that consumption is the measure of production, instead of the contrary, has been the death of every economic theory up to the present.

The veritable solidarity of mankind enables us, indeed, to state with perfect truth that the consumption of each presupposes the consumption of all.

Within the competitive system, the consumption of each presupposes more or less continuously the consumption of all, just as the production of each presupposes the production of all. It is merely a question of how, in what way, this is so. Herr Grün's only answer to this is the moral postulate of human consumption, the recognition of the " essential nature of consumption." Since he knows nothing of the real conditions of production and consumption, he takes refuge in human essence, the last refuge of the true socialists. For the same reason, he insists on proceeding from consumption instead of from production. If you proceed from production, you necessarily concern yourself with the real conditions of production and with the productive activity of men. But if you proceed from consumption, you merely declare that consumption is not at present " human," that it is necessary to cultivate true consumption and so on. Content with this, you can afford to ignore the real living conditions and the activity of men.

It should be mentioned in conclusion that it was precisely those economists who took consumption as their starting-point, who turned out to be reactionary and ignored the revolutionary element in competition and large-scale industry.

(c) *The " Limitations of Papa Cabet."*

Herr Grün concludes his digression on Herr Reybaud and the school of Fourier with the following words:

I wish to make the organizers of labour conscious of their essence, I wish to show them historically where they have sprung from . . . these hybrids . . . who cannot claim as their own even the least of their thoughts. And later, perhaps, I shall find space to make an example of Herr Reybaud, not only of Herr Reybaud but also of Herr Say. The former is, in reality, not so bad, he is merely stupid; but the latter is more than stupid, he is learned.

And so. . . .

The gladiatorial posture into which Herr Grün throws himself, his threats against Reybaud, his contempt for learning, his resounding promises, these are all sure signs that something portentous is stirring within him. Fully " conscious of his essence " as we are, we infer from these symptoms that Herr Grün is on the point of carrying out a most tremendous plagiaristic coup. To anyone who has had experience of his tactics, there is nothing guileless about his bragging; we know it to be entirely a matter of sly calculation.

"And so":

A chapter follows headed:

The organization of labour! Where did this thought originate?—In France.—But how?

It bears the sub-heading:

Review of the eighteenth century.

" Where did this " chapter of Herr Grün's " originate? —In France—But how? " The reader will find out without delay.

It should not be forgotten that Herr Grün wants to make the French organizers of labour conscious of their essence by an historical exposition in the best German style.

"And so."

When Herr Grün realized that Cabet " had his limitations " and that his " mission had long ago fulfilled itself " (which he must have known for a long time), it did not, "of course, mean an end of everything." On the contrary, he laid upon Cabet a new mission; he arbitrarily selects a few quotations from Cabet, strings them together and makes of them the French "background" to Herr Grün's German history of socialist development in the eighteenth century.

How does he set about his task? He reads "productively."

The twelfth and thirteenth chapters of Cabet's *Voyage to Icaria* contain a motley collection of the opinions of ancient and modern authorities in favour of communism. He does not claim that he is tracing an historical movement. The French bourgeois view communism as a suspicious character. Good, says Cabet, in that case, men of the utmost respectability from every age will testify to the good character of my client; and Cabet proceeds exactly like a lawyer. The most incriminating evidence becomes in his hands favourable to his client. One cannot demand historical accuracy in a legal defence. If a famous man happens to let fall a word against money, or inequality, or wealth, or social evils, Cabet seizes upon it, begs him to repeat it, puts it forward as the man's declaration of faith, has it printed, applauds it and cries with ironic good-humour to his irritated bourgeois: "Hear what he has to say! Was he not a communist?" No one escapes him. Montesquieu, Sieyès, Lamartine, even Guizot—communists all in spite of themselves. *Voilà mon communiste tout trouvé!*[33]

Herr Grün is in a productive mood: he reads the quotations collected by Cabet, representing the eighteenth century; he never doubts for a moment the essential rightness of it all; he improvises for the benefit of the reader a mystical connection between the writers whose names happen to occur on one of Cabet's pages, pours over the whole his Young-German literary slops and then gives it the title which we saw above.

"And so."

| Herr Grün :— | Cabet :— |
|---|---|
| Herr Grün introduces his review with the following words : | Cabet introduces his quotations with the following words : |
| "The social idea did not fall from heaven, it is organic, i.e. it arose by a process of gradual development. I cannot write here its complete history, I cannot commence with the Indians and the Chinese and proceed to Persia, Egypt and Judaea. I cannot question the Greeks and Romans about their social consciousness, I cannot take the evidence of Christianity, Neo-Platonism and the Fathers of the Church, I cannot listen to what the Middle Ages and the Arabs have to say, nor can I examine philosophy during the period of its awakening and so on up to the eighteenth century." | " You claim, foes of common ownership, that there is but a scanty weight of opinion in favour of communism. Well then, before your very eyes, I am going to take the evidence of history and of every philosopher. Listen ! I shall not linger to tell you of those peoples of the past who practised or formerly practised community of goods ! Nor shall I linger over the Hebrews . . . nor the Egyptian priesthood, nor Minos . . . Lycurgus and Pythagoras . . . I shall make no mention of Confucius, nor of Zoroaster, who proclaimed, the one in China, the other in Persia, this principle". (*Voyage en Icarie*, 2nd ed., p. 470). |

After the passages given above, Cabet investigates Greek and Roman history, takes the evidence of Christianity, of Neo-Platonism, of the Fathers of the Church, of the Middle Ages, of the Reformation and of philosophy during the period of its awakening. Cf. Cabet, pages 471–82. Herr Grün leaves others " more patient than himself " to copy these eleven pages, " provided their pedantry has left them the necessary humanism to do so " (that is, to copy them). Herr Grün reserves to himself only the social consciousness of the Arabs. We await longingly the disclosures which he has to offer the world. "I must restrict myself to the eighteenth century." Let us follow Herr Grün into the eighteenth century, remarking only that Grün underlines almost the very same words as Cabet.

| Herr Grün :— | Cabet :— |
|---|---|
| Locke, the founder of sensualism, observes: "He whose possessions exceed his needs, oversteps the bounds of reason and of original justice and steals that which belongs to others. *Every surplus is a form of usurpation* and the sight of the needy must prick the conscience of the rich. Ye corrupt ones, who live in the midst of luxury and plenty, tremble for the day when those hapless creatures who have not the necessities of life *shall truly learn what are the rights of man*—deceit, faithlessness and avarice have produced that inequality of possessions *which is the great misfortune of the human race:* piling up all sorts of sufferings, on the one hand beside riches, on the other, beside destitution. *The philosopher must therefore regard the use of money as one of the most pernicious inventions of human industry.*" | But here we have Locke, who exclaims in his admirable *Civil Government*: "He who possesses in excess of his needs, oversteps the bounds of reason and of natural justice *and appropriates the property of others. All excess is usurpation* and the sight of the needy ought to awaken remorse in the soul of the wealthy. Perverse men, you who roll in riches and pleasures, tremble lest one day the wretch who lacks the necessities of life apprehend fully the *rights of man.*" Hear him exclaim again: "Fraud, bad faith, greed, have produced that *inequality of means*, which, by piling on the one hand wealth and vice and on the other poverty and suffering, constitutes *the great misfortune of the human race* [of which Herr Grün makes nonsense]. The philosopher must then regard the use of *money* as one of the most *fatal* discoveries of human industry." Page 485. |

Herr Grün concludes from these quotations of Cabet's that Locke is

> an opponent of the monetary system, a most outspoken opponent of money and of all property which exceeds the limits of need.

Locke was, unfortunately, one of the first scientific champions of the monetary system, a most uncompromising advocate of the flogging of vagabonds and paupers, one of the precursors of modern political economy.

Herr Grün :—
Bossuet the Bishop of Meaux, says in his *Politics derived from Holy Scripture* : " Without governments (without politics)" [an absurd interpolation on the part of Herr Grün] " the earth with all its goods would be the common property of men, just as much as air and light ; no man, according to the original law of nature, has a particular right to anything. *All things are the property of all men; it is from civil government that private property results.*" A priest in the seventeenth century has the honesty to say such things as this, to express such views as these! And the German *Puffendorf*, who is known to us [i.e. to Herr Grün] only through one of Schiller's epigrams, was of the following opinion : " *The*

Cabet :—
Listen to Baron *Puffendorf*, a professor of natural law in Germany and a Councillor of State in Stockholm and Berlin, a man who in his *Law of Nature and Nations* refutes the doctrine of Hobbes and Grotius concerning absolute monarchy, who proclaims natural equality, fraternity, primitive community of goods, and who recognizes property to be a human institution, the result of a distribution of goods, by common consent, to the end that all, and particularly the workers, may be assured of permanent possession, whole or partial, and that in consequence, the existing inequality of possessions is an *injustice* which only involves the other injustices [translated ridiculously by Herr Grün] in

| Herr Grün:— | Cabet:— |
|---|---|
| *present inequality of means is an injustice* which involves all other injustices by reason of the *insolence of the rich and the cowardice* of the poor." Herr Grün adds: "We shall not digress; let us remain in France." | consequence of *the insolence of the rich and the cowardice of the poor.*" And does not Bossuet, the Bishop of Meaux, the preceptor of the French Dauphin, the famous Bossuet, recognize also in his *Politics derived from Holy Scripture* that, were it not for governments, the earth and all possessions would be as common to men as air and light; according to natural law, no one has a particular right to anything; *all things belong to all men* and it is from civil government that property springs. page 486. |

The substance of Herr Grün's digression from France is that Cabet quotes a German. He even spells the German name in the incorrect French fashion. Apart from his occasional mistranslations and omissions, he surprises us by his embellishments. Cabet speaks first of Pufendorf and then of Bossuet, Herr Grün speaks first of Bossuet and then of Pufendorf. Cabet speaks of Bossuet as a famous man; Herr Grün calls him a "priest." Cabet quotes Pufendorf with all his titles; Herr Grün makes the frank admission that he is known only from one of Schiller's epigrams. Now he knows him also from one of Cabet's quotations, and it is apparent that the Frenchman, with all his limitations, has made a closer study than Herr Grün not only of his own countrymen, but of the Germans as well.

Cabet says:

I must make haste to deal with the great philosophers of the eighteenth century; I shall begin with Montesquieu.

In order to reach Montesquieu, Herr Grün begins with a sketch of the "legislative genius of the eighteenth century." Compare their mutual quotations from Montesquieu, Mably, Rousseau, Turgot. It suffices here to compare Cabet and Herr Grün on Rousseau and Turgot. Cabet proceeds from Montesquieu to Rousseau. Herr Grün constructs this transition: "Rousseau was the radical and Montesquieu the constitutional politician."

Herr Grün quotes from Rousseau :—

"The greatest evil has already been done when one finds oneself compelled to defend the poor and restrain the rich, etc.... [ends with the words] hence it follows that the social state is only advantageous to men if they all possess something and none possess too much." According to Herr Grün Rousseau becomes "confused and completely unreliable when he has to answer the question: what transformation does original property undergo when natural man enters into society? What does he answer? He answers: Nature has made all goods common... [ends with the words] in the case of a distribution, the share of each becomes his property."

Cabet :—

Listen now to Rousseau the author of the immortal *Social Contract*—listen : "Men are equal by right. Nature has made all goods common; if distribution takes place the share of each becomes his property. In all cases the sole proprietor of all goods is society" [a point ommitted by Herr Grün]. Listen again : ... [ends] whence it follows that the social state is only advantageous to men in as much as they all have something and that none has too much. Listen, listen again to Rousseau in his *Political Economy* : "The greatest evil has already been done when one has to defend the poor and restrain the rich," etc., etc., pages 489, 490.

Herr Grün makes two ingenious innovations; firstly, he merges the two quotations from the *Social Contract* and the *Political Economy* and secondly he begins where Cabet ends. Cabet names the titles of the writings of Rousseau from which he quotes, Herr Grün suppresses them. The explanation of these tactics is, perhaps, that Cabet is speaking of a *Political Economy*, which Herr Grün does not know, even from an epigram of Schiller. Although Herr Grün is conversant with all the secrets of the *Encyclopédie*, one seems to have escaped his notice: namely, that Rousseau's *Political Economy* is none other than the article in the *Encyclopédie* on political economy.

Let us pass on to Turgot. Herr Grün is not content here with merely copying the quotations; he actually transcribes the sketch that Cabet gives of Turgot.

| Herr Grün :— | Cabet :— |
|---|---|
| One of the noblest and most futile attempts to establish a new order on the foundations of the old, everywhere on the point of collapse, was made by Turgot. It was in vain. The aristocracy brought about an artificial famine, instigated revolts, intrigued and spread calumnies against him until the debonair Louis dismissed his minister. The aristocracy would not listen, therefore it had to suffer. Human development revenges fearfully those good angels who utter the last urgent warning before a catastrophe. The French | Yet while the King declared that he and his minister (Turgot) were the only friends the people had at court, while the people heaped blessings upon him, while the philosophers overwhelmed him with admiration, while Voltaire wished to kiss before he died the hand which had signed so many social improvements, the aristocracy conspired against him, even organized a vast famine, and stirred up insurrections in order to destroy him; by its intrigues and calumnies it succeeded in turning the Paris salons against the reformer and in destroying Louis the |

## TRUE SOCIALISM

Herr Grün:—
people blessed Turgot, Voltaire wished to kiss his hand before he died, the King had called him his friend... Turgot, the Baron, the Minister, one of the last feudal lords, pondered the idea that a domestic press would have to be invented if the freedom of the press were to be completely assured.

Cabet:—
Sixteenth himself by forcing him to dismiss the virtuous minister who could have saved him. [page 497].—Let us return to Turgot, a Baron, a Minister of Louis the Sixteenth during the first year of his reign, one who desired to reform abuses, who carried through a mass of reforms, who wished to establish a new language; a man who actually tried to perfect a household printing press in order to ensure the freedom of the press. page 495.

Cabet calls Turgot a Baron and a Minister, Herr Grün copies this much from him, but by way of improving on Cabet, he changes the youngest son of the provost of the Paris merchants into " one of the oldest of the feudal lords." Cabet is wrong in attributing the famine and the insurrection of 1775 to the machinations of the aristocracy. Up to the present, no one has discovered who was behind the outcry about the famine and the movement connected with it. But in any case popular prejudice and the parliaments themselves had far more to do with it than the aristocracy. It is quite in order for Herr Grün to copy this error of " poor limited Papa " Cabet. He believes in him as in a gospel. On Cabet's authority he numbers Turgot among the communists, Turgot, one of the leaders of the physiocratic school, the most resolute champion of free competition, the defender of usury, the mentor of Adam Smith. Turgot was a great man, for he was adequate to the age in which he lived. He has nothing in common with the imaginings of Herr Grün, the origin of which we have shown already.

Let us now pass to the men of the French Revolution. Cabet greatly embarrasses his bourgeois opponent by numbering Sieyès among the forerunners of communism, by reason of the fact that he recognized equality of rights, and the State as the sole sanction of property (Cabet, page 499–502). Herr Grün, who " is fated to find the French mind inadequate and superficial every time that he comes into close contact with it," copies this with a sigh of relief, and is conceited enough to imagine that an old party leader like Cabet is destined to preserve the " humanism " of Herr Grün from " pedantry." Cabet continues: "Listen to our famous Mirabeau!" Herr Grün says: "Listen to Mirabeau!" and quotes some of the passages stressed by Cabet, in which Mirabeau advocates the equal division of bequeathed property among the relatives. Herr Grün exclaims:

Communism for the family!

On this principle, Herr Grün could go through the whole range of bourgeois institutions, finding in all of them traces of communism, so that taken as a whole they could be said to represent perfect communism. He could christen the *Code Napoléon* a Code of common ownership! And he could discover communist colonies in the brothels, barracks and prisons.

Let us conclude these tiresome quotations with Condorcet. A comparison of the two books will show the reader very clearly how Herr Grün now omits passages, now merges them, now quotes titles, now suppresses them, leaves out the chronological dates but slavishly follows Cabet's order, even when this is chronologically incorrect, and achieves in the end nothing more than an abridgement of Cabet, poorly executed and timidly disguised.

# TRUE SOCIALISM 175

| Herr Grün :— | Cabet :— |
|---|---|
| Condorcet is the radical Girondist. He recognizes the injustice of the distribution of property, he absolves the poor from blame . . . if the people are somewhat dishonest on principle, the cause lies in the institutions themselves. | Listen to Condorcet, who maintained in his reply to the Berlin Academy . . . [a long passage follows in Cabet, concluding] : It is then entirely because the institutions are evil that the people are so frequently a little dishonest on principle. |
| In his journal : *Social Education* . . . he even tolerates large-scale capitalists. . . . | Listen to what he has to say in his journal *Social Education* . . . he even tolerates the existence of large-scale capitalists, etc. |
| Condorcet demanded that the Legislative Assembly should divide the 100 millions, owned by the three princes who emigrated, into 100,000 parts . . . he organized education, and the establishment of public assistance [cf. the original text]. | Listen to one of the Girondist leaders, the philosopher Condorcet, from the tribune of the Legislative Assembly, on the 6th July, 1792 : " Decree that the possessions of the three French princes, Louis the Eighteenth, Charles the Tenth and the Prince of Condé [omitted by Herr Grün], be immediately put up for sale . . . they amount to almost 100 millions, and you will replace three princes by 100 thousand citizens . . . organize education and institutions for public assistance." |
| In his report on public education to the Legisla- | But listen to the Committee of Public Education, presenting to the Legislative Assembly its report on the plan of education |

176          THE GERMAN IDEOLOGY

Herr Grün:— 
tive Assembly, Condorcet says: "The object of education and the duty of the civil authorities is to offer every member of the human race the means of satisfying his needs, etc. [Herr Grün changes the report of the Committee on Condorcet's plan, into a report by Condorcet himself.]

Cabet:—
drawn up by Condorcet, on the 20th April, 1792: "Public education should offer to every individual the means of providing for his needs . . . such ought to be the first aim of national education and from this point of view it is a legal obligation for the civil authorities." pages 502, 503, 505, 509.

Herr Grün, in his efforts to make the French organizers of labour conscious of their essence, by this shameless copying from Cabet, proceeds according to the principle: Divide and rule. He unhesitatingly interpolates among his quotations his considered opinion of persons whom he knows from one passage only, a passage which he had never set eyes on up to a moment before; he also inserts a few phrases on the French Revolution and then divides the whole into two halves by the use of a few quotations from Morelly. Morelly became the fashion in Paris at a moment very opportune for Herr Grün, mainly through the efforts of Villegardelle; the most important passages from his work were translated in the Paris *Vorwärts*[35] long before Herr Grün came upon the scene. We will content ourselves here with one or two glaring examples of Herr Grün's slipshod method of translation.

Morelly: "Self-interest perverts the heart and embitters our dearest ties, changing them into heavy chains; these are the real object of the reciprocal hatred of married couples in this country."

Herr Grün: "Self-interest renders the heart unnatural and pours bitterness upon the dearest ties, which it transforms into heavy chains ; our married people detest them and detest themselves into the bargain."

Utter nonsense.

Morelly : "Our soul contracts so furious a thirst that it chokes in quenching it.

Herr Grün : "Our soul contracts so furious a thirst that it suffocates itself in order to quench it."

Again utter nonsense.

Morelly : "Those who claim to control our morals and dictate our laws, etc."

Herr Grün : "Those who pretend to control our morals and dictate our laws, etc."

Herr Grün makes all three mistakes in the course of fourteen lines, in translating a single passage of Morelly's. In his exposition of Morelly there are also numerous plagiarisms from Villegardelle.

The sum of Herr Grün's knowledge of the eighteenth century and of the Revolution is contained in the following lines :

> Sensualism, deism and theism together stormed the old world. The old world perished. When a new world came to be built, Deism was victorious in the Constituent Assembly, Theism in the Convention, while pure Sensualism was beheaded or deprived of speech.

Here we have the philosophic trick of dismissing history with a few categories proper to ecclesiastical history; Herr Grün reduces it to its basest form, to a mere literary phrase, which serves only to adorn his plagiarisms. *Avis aux philosophes !*[36]

We can ignore Herr Grün's remarks about communism. His historical notes are copied from Cabet's brochures, and the *Voyage to Icaria* is viewed from the standpoint adopted by true socialism (cf. *Bürgerbuch* and *Rhenish Annals*). Herr Grün shows his knowledge of French, and at the same time of English, conditions by calling

Cabet the "communist O'Connell of France," and then says:

> He would be ready to have me hanged if he had the power and knew what I think and write about him. These agitators are dangerous for men such as us, because their intelligence is limited.

### (d) *Proudhon.*

Herr Stein revealed his intellectual poverty in no uncertain way by treating Proudhon lightly (cf. *Einundzwanzig Bogen*, page 84). You need something more than regurgitations of Hegel to follow this logic incarnate.

A few examples may show that Herr Grün remains true to his nature in this section too.

He translates several excerpts from the evidence adduced by Proudhon from political economy to prove that property is inadmissible and finally exclaims:

> We need add nothing to this critique of property; it is the complete liquidation of property. We have no desire to write a new critique, abolishing in its turn equality of production and the isolation of equal workers. I have already indicated what is necessary. The rest [that is, what Herr Grün has not indicated] will be defined when society is rebuilt, when true property-relationships are established.

In this way Herr Grün tries to avoid a close investigation of Proudhon's arguments about political economy and, at the same time, to override them. Proudhon's whole set of proofs is wrong; however, Herr Grün will find the reason why, as soon as someone else has proved it for him. The comments passed in *The Holy Family*[37] on Proudhon, to the effect that Proudhon constructs his political economy from the standpoint of the political economist, and his law from the standpoint of the jurist, are copied by Herr Grün. But he has grasped so little of its meaning that he omits the essential point, that Proudhon vindicates the illusions cherished by jurists and economists concerning their own practice; he offers us instead a set of nonsensical phrases.

The most important thing in Proudhon's *On the Creation of Order in Humanity* is his serial dialectics, the attempt to establish a method of thought in which the process of thinking is substituted for independent thoughts. Proudhon is looking, from the French standpoint, for a dialectic such as Hegel has already given us. A relationship with Hegel is therefore here really in existence; it does not need to be constructed by means of some imaginative analogy. It would have been an easy matter to offer a criticism of Proudhon's dialectic if the criticism of Hegel's had been mastered. But this was hardly to be expected of the true socialists, since the philosopher Feuerbach himself, to whom they defer, did not manage to produce one. Herr Grün makes a ludicrous attempt to shirk his task. At the very moment when he should have brought his heavy German artillery into play, he decamps with an indecent gesture. First of all he fills several pages with translations, and then explains to Proudhon, with bumptious literary *captatio benevolentiae*[38], that his serial dialectics is merely an excuse for showing off his learning. He does indeed try to console him as follows:

> Ah, my dear friend, make no mistake about trying to be a scholar [or tutor]. We have had to forget everything that our pedants and our University hacks [with the exception of Stein, Reybaud and Cabet] have tried to impart to us with such infinite labour and to our mutual disgust.

As a proof that Herr Grün no longer now absorbs knowledge " with such infinite labour," although perhaps with just as much " disgust," we may note that he begins his socialistic studies and letters in Paris on November 6th and by the following January 20th has not only concluded them but has also completed

> ... a cogent exposition of the general impression which they, in their entirety, made upon him.

## 3. "Doctor George Kuhlmann of Holstein," or the Prophecies of True Socialism.[39]

### THE NEW WORLD
### or
### The Kingdom of the Spirit Upon Earth.

*Annunciation.*

A man was needed [so runs the preface] who would give utterance to all our sorrows, all our longings and all our hopes, to everything, in a word, which moves our age most deeply. And it was necessary that he should emerge from the solitude of the spirit into the press and the turmoil of doubts and longings, bearing the solution of the riddle, the living symbols of which encompass us all. This man, whom our age was awaiting, has appeared. He is Dr. George Kuhlmann of Holstein.

August Becker, the writer of these lines, allowed himself to be persuaded, by a person of a very simple mind and very ambiguous character, that not a single riddle has yet been solved, not a single vital energy aroused—that the communist movement, which has already gripped all civilized countries, is an empty nut whose kernel cannot be discovered ; that it is a universal egg, laid by some great universal hen without the aid of a cock—whereas the true kernel and the true cock of the walk is Dr. George Kuhlmann of Holstein ! ...

This great cock of the walk turns out, however, to be a perfectly ordinary capon who has fed for a while on the German artisans in Switzerland and who cannot escape his due fate.[40]

Far be it from us to consider Dr. Kuhlmann of Holstein as a commonplace charlatan and a cunning fraud, who does not himself believe in the efficacy of his elixir and who merely applies his science of longevity to the preservation of life in his own body—no, we are well aware that the inspired doctor is a spiritualistic charlatan, a pious fraud, a mystical swindler, but one who, like all his kind, is none too scrupulous in his choice of means, since his own person is intimately connected with his holy mission. Indeed, holy missions are always bound up with the holy beings who pursue them; for such missions are of a purely idealistic nature and have their being only in the head of the person concerned. All idealists, philosophic and religious, ancient and modern, believe in inspirations, in revelations, saviours, miracle-workers; whether their belief takes a crude religious, or a polished philosophic, form depends only upon their cultural level, just as the degree of energy which they possess, their character, their social position, etc., determine whether their attitude to a belief in miracles is a passive or an active one, i.e. whether they enthral their flock by working miracles or whether they are themselves the sheep who are enthralled; they further determine whether the aims to be pursued are practical or merely theoretical. Kuhlmann is a very energetic person indeed, a man of some philosophic education; his attitude to miracles is by no means a passive one and the aims which he pursues are very practical. All that August Becker has in common with him is the national infirmity of mind. The good fellow " pities those who cannot bring themselves to see that the will and the ideas of an age can only be expressed by individuals." For the idealist, every movement of world importance exists only in the head of some chosen being, and the fate of the world depends on whether this head, which has made all wisdom its own

## 182    THE GERMAN IDEOLOGY

private property, is or is not mortally wounded by some realistic stone before it has had time to make its revelation. "Can it be otherwise?" adds August Becker challengingly.

> Put all the philosophers and the theologians of the age together, let them take counsel and register their votes, and then see what comes of it all!

The whole of historical development consists, according to the ideologist, in those theoretical abstractions which originate in the "heads" of "all the philosophers and theologians of the age," and since it is impossible to "put" all these "heads together" and induce them to "take council and register their votes," there must of necessity be one sacred head, the spear-head of all these philosophical and theological heads, in a word, the speculative unity of all these blockheads—the saviour.

This "cranium" system is as old as the Egyptian pyramids, with which it has many similarities, and as new as the Prussian monarchy, in the capital of which it has recently been resurrected, as young as ever. The idealistic Dalai Lamas have this much in common with their real counterpart: they would like to persuade themselves that the world from which they derive their subsistence could not continue without their holy excrement. As soon as this idealistic folly is put into practice, its malevolent nature is apparent: its monkish lust for power, its religious fanaticism, its charlatanry, its pietistic hypocrisy, its unctuous deceit. Miracles are the asses' bridge leading from the kingdom of the idea to practice. Dr. George Kuhlmann of Holstein is just such an asses' bridge—he is inspired—his magic words cannot fail to move the most stable of mountains. How consoling for those patient creatures who cannot summon up enough energy to blast the mountain with natural powder! What a source of confidence to the blind and timorous who cannot see the material coherence which underlies the manifold fractions of the revolutionary movement. "There has been lacking, up to now, a rallying point," says August Becker.

Saint George overcomes all concrete obstacles with the greatest of ease by transforming all concrete things into ideas; he then assumes himself to be the speculative unity of the latter, an assumption which enables him to " rule and regulate them " :

> The society of ideas is the world. And its unity regulates and rules the world.

Our prophet wields all the power he can possibly desire in this " society of ideas."

> Let us then wander, led by our own idea, hither and thither, and contemplate all things in the minutest detail, as far as our age shall demand it.

What a speculative unity of nonsense!

But paper is long-suffering, and the German public, to whom the prophet issues his oracles, knows so little of the philosophic development in its own country, that it does not even notice how, in his speculative prophecies, our great prophet merely reiterates the most decrepit philosophic phrases and adapts them to his practical aims.

Just as medical miracle workers and miraculous cures are made possible by ignorance of the laws of the natural world, social miracle-workers and miraculous social cures thrive upon ignorance of the laws of the social world—and the witch-doctor of Holstein is none other than the socialistic miracle-working shepherd of Niederempt.

The first revelation which this miracle-working shepherd makes to his flock is as follows:

I see before me an assembly of the elect, who have gone before me to work by word and deed for the salvation of our time, and who are now come to hear what I have to say concerning the weal and woe of mankind.

Many have already spoken and written in the name of mankind, but none has yet given utterance to the real nature of man's suffering, his hopes and his expectations, nor told him how he may obtain his desires. That is precisely what I shall do.

And his flock believes him.

There is not a single original thought in the whole work of this "Holy Spirit"; he reduces out-of-date socialistic theories to abstractions of the most sterile and general kind. There is nothing original even in the form, the style. Others have imitated more happily the sanctified style of the Bible. Kuhlmann has taken Lamennais as his model, but he merely achieves a caricature of Lamennais. We shall give our readers a sample of the beauties of his style:

Tell me firstly, how feel ye when ye think on your eternal lot?

Many indeed mock and say: What have I to do with eternity?

Others rub their eyes and ask: Eternity—what may this be?

How feel ye, further, when ye think on the hour when the grave shall swallow you up?

And I hear many voices. [One among them speaks in this wise:]

Of recent years it hath been taught that the spirit is eternal, that in death it is only dissolved once more in God, from whom it proceedeth. But they who preach such things cannot tell me what then remaineth of me. Oh, that I had never seen the light of day! And assuming that I do not die—oh, my parents, my sisters, my brothers, my children, and all whom I love, shall I ever see you again? Oh, had I but never seen you! etc.

How feel ye, further, if ye think on infinity? ... "

We feel very poorly, Herr Kuhlmann—not at the thought of death but at your idea of death, at your style, at the underhand means you employ to work upon the feelings of others.

" How dost feel," dear reader, when you hear a priest painting hell very hot and making minds very flabby, a priest whose eloquence only aims at stimulating the tear glands of his hearers and who speculates on the cowardice of his congregation?

As far as the meagre content of the " Annunciation " is concerned, the first section, or the introduction to the " New World," can be reduced to the simple thought that Herr Kuhlmann has come from Holstein to found the " Kingdom of the Spirit," the " Kingdom of Heaven " upon earth; that he was the first to know the real heaven and the real hell—the latter being society as it has hitherto existed and the former being future society, the " Kingdom of the Spirit "—and that he himself is the longed-for holy " Spirit " ...

Saint George is not the first to have such thoughts, and there was really no need for him to have toiled all the way from Holstein to Switzerland, nor to have descended from the " solitude of the Spirit " to the level of the artisans, nor to have " revealed " himself, merely in order to present this " vision " to the " world."

However the idea that Dr. Kuhlmann of Holstein is the " longed-for Holy Spirit " is his own exclusive property—and is likely to remain so.

The content of Saint George's Holy Scripture, according to his own " revelation," is as follows:

> It will reveal to you [he says] the Kingdom of the Spirit in its earthly guise, that ye may behold its glory and see that there is no other salvation but in the Kingdom of the Spirit. On the other hand it will set before you your vale of tears that ye may behold

your wretchedness and know the cause of all your sufferings. Then I shall show the way which leads from this sorrowful present to a joyful future. To this end, follow me in the spirit to a height, whence we may have a free prospect over the broad landscape.

And so the prophet permits us first of all a glimpse of his " beautiful landscape," his Kingdom of Heaven. We see nothing but a misunderstanding of Saint-Simonism, wretchedly staged, with costumes that are a travesty of Lamennais, embellished with fragments from Herr Stein.

We shall now quote the most important revelations of the Kingdom of Heaven, a vindication of the prophetic method. For example :

> Ye may choose freely and according to your several inclinations. Inclination will follow from one's natural faculties.
> If in society [Saint George prophesies] each man follows his inclination, all faculties will be developed as a whole and if this is so, that which all need as a whole will continually be produced, in the realm of the spirit as in the realm of matter. For society always possesses as many faculties and energies as it has needs. *Les attractions sont proportionelles aux destinées,*[41] [Cf. also Proudhon].

Herr Kuhlmann differs here from the socialists and the communists only by reason of a misunderstanding, the cause of which must be sought in his pursuit of practical aims and doubtless in his limitations. He confuses the diversity of faculties and capacities with the inequality of possessions and enjoyment conditioned by possession, and inveighs therefore against communism:

> No one shall have there [that is, under communism] any advantage over another, [declaims the prophet] no one shall have more possessions and live better than another . . . and if you cherish doubts about it and

fail to join in their outcry, they will abuse you, condemn you, and persecute you and hang you on a gallows.

Kuhlmann sometimes prophesies quite correctly, one must admit.

In their ranks are to be found all those who cry : Away with the Bible ! Away, above all, with the Christian religion, the religion of humility and servility ! Away with all belief whatsoever ! We know nothing of God or immortality ! They are but figments of the imagination, exploited and continually concocted by deceivers and liars for their own advantage [he means, which are exploited by the priests for their own advantage]. In sooth, he who still believes in such is the greatest of fools !

Kuhlmann attacks with particular vehemence the opponents of the doctrine of faith, humility and inequality, i.e. the doctrine of " difference of class and of birth." He founds his socialism on the abject doctrine of predestined slavery, which reminds one strongly, as Kuhlmann formulates it, of Friedrich Rohmer—on the theocratic hierarchy and in the last instance on his own sacred person !

Every branch of labour [we find] is controlled by the most skilled worker, who himself takes part in it, and every branch of enjoyment is controlled by the most contented member, who himself participates in the enjoyment. But, as society is undivided and possesses only one mind, the whole scheme of things will be regulated and governed by one man—and he shall be the wisest, the most virtuous and the most blissful.

On page 34 we learn :

If man strives after virtue in the spirit, then he is active and moves his limbs and develops and moulds and forms everything in and outside himself according to his pleasure. And if he experiences well-being in the spirit, then he must also experience it in everything that moves and has its being in him. Therefore, man shall eat and drink and take delight therein; therefore he shall sing and play, he shall kiss, weep and laugh.

The knowledge of the influence which the vision of God exerts on the appetite, and which spiritual blissfulness exerts upon the sex impulse is, of course, not the private property of Kuhlmann; but it sheds light on many an obscure passage in the prophet.

For example:

Both [possession and enjoyment] conform to his labour [that is, to man's labour]. This is the measure of his needs. [In this way, Kuhlmann distorts the claim that a communist society has, on the whole, always as many natural faculties and energies as needs.] For labour is the expression of the ideas and the instincts. And therein needs are contained. But, since the faculties and needs of men are always different, and so apportioned that the former only can be developed and the latter satisfied, if each continually labours for all and the product of the labour of all be exchanged and apportioned in accordance with the deserts (!) of each—for this reason each receives only the value of his labour.

The whole of this tautological rigmarole would be—like the following sentences and many others which we spare the reader—utterly incomprehensible, despite the " sublime simplicity and clarity " of the " revelation " so praised by A. Becker, if we had not a key in the shape of the practical aims which the prophet is pursuing. This makes everything at once comprehensible.

Value [prophesies Herr Kuhlmann further] will correspond to the need of all. (?) In value the work of each is always contained and for it (?) he can procure for himself whatever his heart desires.

## TRUE SOCIALISM

See, my friends [runs page 39], the society of true men envisages life always as a school . . . in which man must educate himself. And it must help him, too, to attain bliss. But such (?) must manifest itself and become visible (?), otherwise it (?) is impossible.

Herr George Kuhlmann asserts then that " such " (life ? or bliss ?) must " manifest itself " and become " visible," because " it " would otherwise be " impossible "—that " labour " is " contained in value " and that one can procure for it (for what ?) one's heart's desire—and finally, that " value " will correspond to " need." It would be impossible to fathom his meaning unless one once again takes into account the point of the whole revelation, the practical basis of it all.

Let us therefore try to offer a practical explanation.

Saint George Kuhlmann of Holstein was a prophet without honour in his own country. He arrives in Switzerland and finds there an entirely " New World," the communist societies of the German artisans. That is exactly what he wants—and he attaches himself without delay to communism and the communists. He always, as August Becker tells us, " worked unremittingly to develop his doctrine further and to make it adequate to the greatness of the times," i.e. he became a communist among the communists *ad majorem Dei gloriam*.[42] So far everything had gone well. But one of the most vital principles of communism, a principle which distinguishes it from all reactionary socialism, is its empiric view, based on a knowledge of men, that differences of brain, of intellectual capacity, do not imply any difference whatsoever in the nature of the stomach and of physical needs ; therefore the false tenet, based upon existing circumstances, " to each according to his capacity," must be changed, in so far as it relates to enjoyment in its narrower sense, into the tenet, " to each according to his need"; in other words, a different form of activity, of labour, confers no privileges in respect of possession and enjoyment. The prophet could not admit this; for the privileges, the advantages of his station, the feeling that he is one of the elect, these are the very stimulus of the prophet. "But such things must be made manifest and be visible, otherwise it is impossible." Without practical advantages, without some tangible stimulus, the prophet would not be a prophet at all, he would not be a practical, but only a theoretical, man of God, a philosopher. The prophet must therefore make the communists understand that different forms of activity or labour give the right to different degrees of value and of bliss (or of enjoyment, merit, pleasure, and all the rest of it) and since each determines his own bliss and his labour, therefore he, the prophet—this is the practical point of the revelation —can claim a better life than the common artisan.\* After this, all the prophet's obscurities become clear: now we see why the " possession " and " enjoyment " of each should correspond to his " labour "; why the " labour " of man should be the measure of his " needs "; why, therefore, each should receive the " value " of his work; why " value " will determine itself according to " need "; why the work of each is " contained " in value and why he can procure for it what his " heart " desires; why, finally, the " bliss " of the chosen one must " be made manifest and become visible," because it is otherwise " impossible." All this nonsense now acquires a meaning.

We do not know the exact extent of the practical demands which Dr. Kuhlmann makes upon the artisans. But we do know that his doctrine is a dogma fundamental to all spiritual and temporal craving for power,

---

\*The prophet openly admits this in a lecture which has not been printed.

a mystic veil which obscures all furtive, hypocritical pleasure-seeking, we know that it serves to extenuate any infamy and that it is the source of much mental derangement.

We must not omit to show the reader the way, which, according to Herr Kuhlmann of Holstein, "leads out of the sorrowful present to a joyous future." This way is lovely and delightful as a flowery meadow in spring.

> Softly and gently, with sun-warmed fingers, buds burgeon, the lark and the nightingale warble, the grasshopper in the grass is roused. Let the new world therefore come like the spring.

The prophet paints the transition from present social isolation to communal life in truly idyllic colours. We remember how he transformed real society into a "society of ideas," so that "he could wander hither and thither, led by his own idea, and contemplate everything in its smallest details, to the extent that the age demanded it"; in the same way he transforms the real social movement which already, in all civilized countries, proclaims the approach of a terrible social upheaval—into a process of comfortable and peaceful conversion, a still-life which will permit the owners and rulers of the world to slumber on in complete peace of mind. For the idealist, the theoretical abstractions of real events, their ideal signs, are reality—real events are merely "signs that the old world is going to its doom."

> Wherefore do ye strive so furiously for the things of the moment [scolds the prophet], they are nothing more than signs that the old world is going to its doom; and wherefore do ye dissipate your strength in strivings which cannot fulfil your hopes and expectations?
> Ye shall not tear down nor destroy that which ye

find in your path, ye shall rather go out of your way to avoid it and pass it by. And when ye have avoided it and passed it by, then it shall cease to exist of itself, for it shall find no other nourishment.

If ye seek truth and spread light abroad, then lying and darkness will vanish from your midst.

But there will be many who will say: "How shall we build a new life as long as the old order prevails and hinders us? Must it not first be destroyed?" "In no wise," answers the sagest, the most virtuous and the most blissful. "In no wise. If ye dwell with others in a house that has become rotten and is too small and uncomfortable for you, and the others wish to remain in it, then ye shall not pull it down and dwell in the open, but ye shall first build a new house, and when it is ready ye shall enter it and abandon the old to its fate."

The prophet now gives two pages of rules as to how one can insinuate oneself into the new world. Then he becomes aggressive:

But it is not enough that ye should stand together and forsake the old world—ye shall also take arms against it to make war upon it and to extend your kingdom and strengthen it. Not by the use of force, however, but rather by the use of free persuasion.

But if one finds oneself forced, after all, to take up a real sword and hazard one's real life " to conquer heaven by force of arms," the prophet promises his sacred host a Russian immortality (the Russians believe that they will rise again in their respective localities if they are killed in battle by the enemy):

And they who shall fall by the wayside shall be born anew and shall rise more beauteous than they were before. Therefore (therefore!) take no thought for your life and fear not death.

And so the prophet bids his sacred host be calm, even at the prospect of a conflict with real weapons;

you do not really risk your life; you merely pretend to risk it.

The prophet's doctrine is in every sense sedative. After these samples of his Holy Scripture one cannot wonder at the applause it has met with among certain drowsy and easy-going readers.

## APPENDIX

## THESES ON FEUERBACH

THE famous eleven Theses on Feuerbach were found by Engels in an old note-book of Marx's, forty years after they were written. (See Engels' Preface to *Feuerbach and the Outcome of Classical German Philosophy*, 1886.) They were not in a finished form and Engels published them in a more polished shape, in which they are well known to all students of Marxism.

The original Theses were first published in 1932 in the *Marx-Engels Gesamtausgabe* I.5, and offer a number of interesting variations from the Engels' version; they can be compared with the best English translation of the Engels' version, that edited by C. P. Dutt, in Engels' *Feuerbach and the Outcome of Classical German Philosophy* (Lawrence & Wishart Ltd.).

## Theses on Feuerbach

### I

The chief defect of all materialism up to now (including Feuerbach's) is, that the object, reality, what we apprehend through our senses, is understood only in the form of the *object* or *contemplation*;[1] but not as *sensuous human activity*, as *practice*; not subjectively. Hence in opposition to materialism the *active* side was developed abstractly by idealism—which of course does not know real sensuous activity as such. Feuerbach wants sensuous objects, really distinguished from the objects of thought: but he does not understand human activity itself as *objective* activity.[2] Hence, in *The Essence of Christianity*, he sees only the theoretical attitude as the true human attitude, while practice is understood and established only in its "dirty Jew" appearance. He therefore does not comprehend the significance of "revolutionary," of "practical-critical" activity.

### II

The question whether objective truth is an attribute of human thought—is not a theoretical but a *practical* question. Man must prove the truth, i.e. the reality and power, the "this-sidedness" of his thinking in practice. The dispute over the reality or non-reality of thinking that is isolated from practice is a purely *scholastic* question.

### III

The materialistic doctrine concerning the changing of circumstances and education forgets that circumstances are changed by men and that the educator himself must be educated. This doctrine has therefore to divide society into two parts, one of which is superior to society.

The coincidence of the changing of circumstances and of human activity or self-changing can only be comprehended and rationally understood as *revolutionary practice*.

### IV

Feuerbach starts out from the fact of religious self-estrangement,³ of the duplication of the world into a religious and a secular one. His work consists in resolving the religious world into its secular basis. But that the secular basis raises itself above itself and establishes for itself an independent realm in the clouds can be explained only through the cleavage and self-contradictions within this secular basis. The latter must therefore in itself be both understood in its contradiction and revolutionized in practice. Therefore after, e.g., the earthly family is discovered to be the secret of the heavenly family, one must proceed to destroy the former both in theory and in practice.

### V

Feuerbach, not satisfied with *abstract thought*, wants contemplation: but he does not understand our sensuous nature as *practical*, human-sensuous activity.

### VI

Feuerbach resolves the essence of religion into the essence of *man*. But the essence of man is no abstraction inherent in each separate individual. In its reality it is the *ensemble* (aggregate) of social relations.

Feuerbach, who does not enter more deeply into the criticism of this real essence, is therefore forced:

1. To abstract[4] from the process of history and to establish the religious temperament as something independent, and to postulate an abstract—*isolated*—human individual.
2. The essence of man can therefore be understood only as "genus," the inward, dumb generality which *naturally* unites the many individuals.

### VII

Feuerbach therefore does not see that the "religious temperament" itself is a social product and that the abstract individual whom he analyses belongs to a particular form of society.

### VIII

All social life is essentially *practical*. All the mysteries which urge theory into mysticism find their rational solution in human practice and in the comprehension of this practice.

### IX

The highest point to which contemplative materialism can attain, i.e. that materialism which does not comprehend our sensuous nature as practical activity, is the contemplation of separate individuals and of civil society.[5]

### X

The standpoint of the old type of materialism is civil society, the standpoint of the new materialism is human society or social humanity.

### XI

The philosophers have only *interpreted* the world differently, the point is, to *change* it.

## NOTES

### FEUERBACH

[1] Ludwig Feuerbach.
[2] Bruno Bauer.
[3] Max Stirner.
[4] The successors of Alexander the Great.
[5] " Worthless residue."
[6] *Voraussetzung.* Normally a theoretical " pre-supposition," Marx uses it in the sense of the real conditions under which a process develops. In *Capital* the term is usually translated " pre-requisite " but this does not give the full meaning of the term in this early work. Marx here deliberately uses the philosophic term and infuses into it a new, material content.
[7] *Subsumieren.* A term of logic meaning " to include as a member within a class." In accordance with his general method, Marx uses this term in a materialistic sense, applying it e.g. to men and the social class under which they are " subsumed."
[8] Max Stirner, to whom Marx gives the nickname " Saint-Max " (as Bruno Bauer—" Saint Bruno "), because he interprets material relationships as spiritual.
[9] " Human " is Feuerbach's slogan; " critical " Bauer's; " egoistic " Stirner's.
[10] *Verkehr.* The word, as used by Marx, means " intercourse," with a slight flavour of " commercial " intercourse. I have usually used the word intercourse, but it must be remembered that the word means intercourse based on economic needs; in one or two places the word " commerce " seemed more correct (cf. the earlier use of "commerce" which originally meant social intercourse in general, and only later meant commercial intercourse).
[11] *Mobiles* and *immobiles Privateigentum.* The technical translation is " personal property " and " real property " (or " personalty " and " realty "). In a non-technical work, however, these terms are confusing, and I have preferred " movable " and " immovable " (for which there is good authority). For Marx in this work " movable property " is that which can be estimated in terms of money and turned into money; " immovable " cannot be so transformed.
[12] *Naturwüchsig* (" growing naturally "). Marx's use of this term seems not quite consistent. He uses it (p. 20) to distinguish the economic development of pre-capitalistic times, where the division of labour is determined by " natural pre-dispositions," e.g. physical strength, needs, accidents, etc. On pp. 47 and 51 similarly, where " natural " capital is attached to the labour and inherited environment of a guildsman, as opposed to the capital of the modern capitalist, which is movable and can be assessed

## NOTES

in terms of money. But elsewhere (pp. 22, 63) " natural " society is one in which there is a cleavage between the particular and the common interest, hence where men have no control over themselves or society. To this " natural " society he opposes communist society with its planning (p. 70, ff.).

[13] The Licinian agrarian law, passed 367 B.C. limited the amount of common land which a single Roman citizen could hold, and is a sign of the growth of private ownership in Rome.

[14] *Ständisches Eigentum*, property inseparable from the *Stand*, the social estate to which the owner belonged.

[15] An instrument perfected in the late Middle Ages, to throw, by means of mirrors, an image of a scene on a plane surface. It was widely used by artists to establish the correct proportions of a natural object or scene. The image appeared on the paper inverted; though the later use of a lens corrected this.

[16] Bruno Bauer.

[17] *Moment*. A philosophic term which means " a determining active factor."

[18] *Naturwüchsig*—see note 12 above.

[19] See note 12 above.

[20] *Die Deutsch-Französischen Jahrbücher*, Paris 1844, edited jointly by Marx and Ruge. The reference is particularly to Marx's articles *On the Jewish Question* and *A Contribution to the Critique of the Hegelian Philosophy of Law*.

[21] *Die Heilige Familie* . . . by Marx and Engels, Frankfurt, 1845.

[22] The sentence is imperfect in the original.

[23] *Entfremdung*. In the *German Ideology* Marx makes his final reckoning with this concept of " self-estrangement."

For Hegel, the development of society, which is the mode of self-development of the Absolute Idea, occurs through the projection of mind into matter, the self-estrangement of mind in a material form alien to its true nature. Through the struggle between mind and its estranged form higher forms are produced. The process of self-estrangement is the very form of existence of mind, leading to the final stage of absolute knowledge. This concept, which bears the essence of Hegel's idealism and dialectics, is transformed by the Young-Hegelians into the idea of the loss of man, in modern society, of the " essence " of man, his deprivation of a full life, of true justice, freedom, etc. In the works of 1844 Marx wrestles with this concept, and charges it with a new content. The " self-estrangement " of Absolute Mind, or of human essence, comes to be for him an idealistic and perverted expression for the real cleavage of society into classes, for the exploitation of the workers by the owners of property. He makes the conclusion, that to abolish " self-estrangement " one must abolish private property.

The following passages illustrate Marx's use of the concept :

The possessing class and the class of the proletariat represent

NOTES

the same human self-estrangement. But the former is comfortable in this self-estrangement and finds therein its own confirmation, knows that this self-estrangement is its own power, and possesses in it the semblance of a human existence. The latter feels itself annihilated in this self-estrangement, sees in it its impotence and the reality of an inhuman existence (*Holy Family*, Chap. 4).

How does it come about that personal interests continually grow, despite the persons, into class-interests, into common interests which win an independent existence over against the individual persons, in this independence take on the shape of general interests, enter as such into opposition with the real individuals, and in this opposition, according to which they are defined as general interests, can be conceived by the consciousness as ideal, even as religious, sacred interests ? How does it come about that, within this process of the self-assertion of personal interests as class-interests, the personal behaviour of the individual must become hard and remote, *estranged* from itself, and at the same time exists apart from him as an independent power produced by intercourse, transforms itself into social relations, into a series of powers which determine and subordinate him and hence seem conceptually to be " sacred " powers ? (*Ideology*—" Saint Max," *Gesamtausgabe*, I, 5, p. 226).

[24] Should " England " be put for " France " and " France " for " England " ? Marx gives a masterly account of the historical process by which landed property in England went out of the hands of the many into those of the few in *Capital*, vol. II, Chaps. XXVII–XXIX.

[25] *Bürgerliche Gesellschaft*. This term is often wrongly translated as "bourgeois society." On the one hand it has the meaning of "civilized society," i.e. society with government, laws, etc., as opposed to "natural" or primitive society ; and also serves to denote the personal and economic relations of men as opposed to political relations and forms. In particular it arose and was used in the seventeenth and eighteenth centuries amongst bourgeois theoreticians as a theoretical attack on political forms which prevented the free accumulation of private property. Cf. such terms as civil law, i.e. law which regulates the relations between individuals, as opposed to public law, which regulates the relations between the State and public bodies. The present context indicates the faultiness of the rendering "bourgeois society."

[26] Bruno Bauer and Max Stirner.

[27] *Die Hallischen Jahrbücher für deutsche Wissenschaft und Kunst*, Leipzig, 1838–41, and *Die Deutschen Jahrbücher für Wissenschaft und Kunst*, Leipzig, 1841–2. These were the chief organs of the Young-Hegelians ; both were edited by Arnold Ruge.

[28] " Theatre of the world."

## NOTES

[29] Bruno Bauer—*Geschichte der Politik, Cultur und Aufklärung des 18ten Jahrhunderts.* Charlottenburg, 1843 and 1845.

[30] Ludwig Feuerbach—*Grundsätze der Philosophie der Zukunft*, 1843.

[31] The words in brackets are suggested by the editor of the *Gesamtausgabe* to fill in a gap in the MS.

[32] Marx sums up his criticism of Feuerbach in the famous *Theses on Feuerbach*, see pp. 195–199.

[33] By " theodicy " is meant a proof of the justice and goodness of God, cf. Leibniz's *Theodicy*.

[34] *Naturwüchsig*—see note 12 above.

[35] *Ständisches Kapital*—see note 14 above.

[36] See note 11 above.

[37] *Naturwüchsig-ständisches Kapital*—see note 12, and note 14 above.

[38] See note 11 above.

[39] *Recht*. This word, often translated as " right," means both system or theory of law, and right. It is opposed to *Gesetz*, a positive law (see page 60).

[40] " Full ownership in accordance with the law."

[41] " The right of using and consuming."

[42] The primitive economy in which men merely collected and hunted natural produce.

[43] *Selbstbetätigung*—by this term Marx means activity which derives from and develops further the natural capacities and talents of men.

[44] *Naturwüchsigkeit*—see note 12 above.

[45] See note 23 above.

[46] Cf. the passage in " Saint Max," the second section of the *Ideology* : " Stirner says ' a society cannot be renewed as long as those who compose and constitute it remain the same as ever.'

"Stirner believes that the communist proletarians, who are revolutionizing society, putting the relations of production and the form of intercourse on a new basis—i.e. on the new men, on their new mode of life—remain ' the same as ever.' The untiring propaganda which these proletarians are making, the discussions which they carry on daily among themselves, prove sufficiently how little they want to remain ' the same as ever,' and how little altogether they want men to remain ' the same as ever.' They would only remain ' the same as ever ' if, with Saint-Sancho (Stirner) they were ' to seek the guilt in themselves ' ; but they know too well that only under changed circumstances will they cease to be ' the same as ever,' and therefore they are determined to change their circumstances at the first opportunity. In revolutionary activity, change of self coincides with the change of circumstances " (*Gesamtausgabe*, I. 5, p. 193). See also the *Theses on Feuerbach*, Thesis 3.

[47] " Against man." Stirner had opposed the idea of men setting themselves an aim or goal, adducing the example of dogs

NOTES

and sheep who do not strive towards an ideal form of dog or sheep.

[48] " In spite of themselves."
[49] *Naturwüchsig*—see note 12 above.
[50] J.-J. Rousseau—*Du contrat social*, 1762. The remark in the text applies to the whole idea of a social contract, i.e. a voluntary decision of individuals to combine in a society.

TRUE SOCIALISM.

[1] Not included in this translation.
[2] An article bearing this title in the *Rheinische Jahrbücher*, 1845, vol. I (by F. H. Semmig). Marx and Engels take this, and the article " Cornerstones of Socialism " (by R. Mathäi) in the same volume, as typical of certain trends in " true socialism."
[3] By " anthropology " is meant Feuerbach's doctrine.
[4] Parodied from Heine, *Lyrisches Intermezzo*, 1822-3, No. 50 :

> With gaping jaws the canon cries
> " Too crude love must not be,
> Or you'll get an infirmity "—
> " How so ? " the maiden sighs.

[5] " Touch me not."
[6] Fr. J. de Chastellux—*La félicité publique*, 1772.
[7] P-H-D. d'Holbach—*Système de la nature*, 1770-1.
[8] *La démocratie pacifique*, a daily newspaper, organ of the disciples of Fourier. In the *Holy Family* Engels says of its " watered-down Fourierism " that it was nothing but " the social doctrine of a part of the philanthropic bourgeoisie."
[9] *Le Populaire* was the organ of Cabet.
[10] *Rentiers*—those who live on investments.
[11] " All brothers, all friends."
[12] From Heine, *Zeitgedichte*, 1844, *Verkehrte Welt*.
[13] " Gold is but a chimera."
[14] From Heine, *Deutschland ein Wintermärchen*, 1844, Caput VII.
[15] " We are banned from earth, water, air and fire."
[16] " The war of all against all."
[17] The word " construction " is used here, as elsewhere in the works of Marx and Engels, to denote a chain of ideas, supposed to be logical, which would claim to explain a material process.
[18] Marx and Engels—*Die Heilige Familie*, 1845.
[19] G. W. F. Hegel—*Rechtsphilosophie*, 1833, p. 248.
[20] The " organization of labour " was the main slogan of the democratic socialist party in France, the leaders of which were Louis Blanc, Ledru-Rollin, and Ferdinand Flocon. The text may refer to Fourier's theory of the organization of labour, according to which society is best served by an organization of labour based on the fullest satisfaction of the " passions " (*Théorie de l'unité universelle*, vol. I).
[21] The " Young Germany " referred to is not the confusedly

P

## NOTES

radical, atheistic and humanitarian group in Switzerland in the early 1840's, but a few middle-class reformers of the 1830's. Under the stimulus of the July Revolution in France and guided by the writings of Saint-Simon, Börne and Heine, a group of writers tried to popularize in Germany certain liberal ideas. Partly owing to their own tastes, partly owing to the severity of the censorship, they covered up their social ideas under a sugary coating of literary elegance, imitating in a feeble way the style of Heine. The most notable of them were Gutzkow, Laube and Mundt. After the banning of their past and future (!) writings in 1835 most of them became petty fashionable littérateurs. Engels acknowledged some indebtedness to them in his earliest work.

[22] Hess had written (*Einundzwanzig Bogen*, p. 88), " we have still to await a work which gives us the historical development of communism."

[23] The reference is to the hackneyed lines of the Swiss physiologist A. von Haller : " Into the heart of nature no created spirit can penetrate. Fortunate is he to whom she shows her outward shell." The lines are characteristic of the mechanism and idealism of the philosophy of nature of the early eighteenth century.

[24] The famous line from Schiller's *Robbers*, 1781.

[25] *L'Organisateur* was the periodical of the Saint-Simonists, 1819 ff.

[26] The " national domains " were the lands and rights of the French royal house which passed into the possession of the State following the French Revolution of 1789. The main part of this property, together with the confiscated property of the Church, was thrown on to the market under the name of " biens nationaux," and gave rise to much speculation.

[27] The Newton Council was a scheme of Saint-Simon's for liberating scientists and artists to dispose freely of their talents. " Open a subscription before the tomb of Newton ; all may subscribe as much and as little as they please. Every subscriber should nominate three mathematicians, three physicists, three chemists, three physiologists, three writers, three painters, three musicians. Every year the subscription and nomination are renewed, with power of changing as each wishes. Share the sum of the subscriptions among the three mathematicians, the three physicists, etc., who will have received the most votes. . . . Those who are nominated must engage themselves to accept no positions, honours or money from any set or party of the subscribers, and are left individually absolutely free to employ their talents as they think fit " (*Lettres d'un habitant de Genève*, I).

[28] *Le Producteur* 1825–6, a weekly organ of the disciples of Saint-Simon. For *L'Organisateur*, see note 25 above.

[29] *Le Globe*, a periodical founded in 1824, was put at the service of the Saint-Simonists from 1831 to 1832. The editor, Pierre Leroux, later developed an abstract equalitarian theory of his own.

NOTES

[30] *Die Hallischen Jahrbücher*—see note 27, *Feuerbach*.

[31] The style of the preceding quotation from Grün is an imitation of Heine.

[32] The reference is to Marx's article *On the Jewish Question* in the *Deutsch-Französische Jahrbücher* (see note 20, *Feuerbach*).

[33] " There's your communist all complete."

[34] I have not been able to identify Cabet's quotation from Locke. The passage seems rather to be a free rendering of certain parts of Locke's two essays, *On Government* and *On Civil Government*, see especially Chap. IV of the former.

[35] *Vorwärts* was the periodical run by German émigrés in Paris, 1844–5. It was suppressed by Guizot at the instance of the Prussian Government. Marx contributed one article to it.

[36] " A warning to the philosophers."

[37] See note 18.

[38] " Attempt to win goodwill."

[39] This section was written probably by Moses Hess, who had been convinced by Marx and Engels that their criticism of " true socialism " was justified. It was edited by Marx.

[40] Marx refers to the communist League of the Just, an organization of German artisans in Switzerland founded by Weitling on the model of the Paris League of the Just.

[41] " There are as many attractions as destinies," i.e. the needs and demands of society are proportional to the supply of human faculties and talents.

[42] " To the greater glory of God."

### Theses on Feuerbach

[1] *Anschauung*. I have used "contemplation" for this term. This, the normal translation, is somewhat ambiguous, and should be understood as "sense-perception," in strong contrast to its meaning of "meditation." In Thesis 9 the translation of the Marx-Engels-Lenin Institute puts, also, "outlook" for *Anschauung*, which seems incorrect in this context.

[2] "Activity through objects."

[3] See note 23 *Feuerbach*, above.

[4] *Abstrahieren* (to abstract) means, in Feuerbach's own words: " to place the essence of nature outside nature, the essence of man outside man, the essence of thought outside the act of thinking " (*Vorläufige Thesen zu einer Reform der Philosophie*, 1843.)

[5] See note 25, *Feuerbach*, above.

# INDEX OF AUTHORS AND WORKS REFERRED TO IN *THE GERMAN IDEOLOGY*

Aikin, John (1747–1822). English doctor, historian and radical publicist. *Description of the country from thirty to forty miles round Manchester.* 1795.

*Anekdota*—a collection of articles forbidden by the Prussian censorship, ed. A. Ruge, Switzerland, 1843 (see Feuerbach).

Babœuf, F. N. (1760–97). An early French communist, guillotined during the French Revolution for conspiring to establish a communist social order.

Barmby, Goodwin (1820–81). English Christian socialist.

Barrère, Bertrand (1775–1841). French republican politician. *Le point du jour, ou Résultat de ce qui s'est passé la veille à l'Assemblée nationale 1789–91*, ed. Barrère.

Bauer, Bruno (1809–82) (See Introduction). *Kritik der evangelischen Geschichte der Synoptiker*, 1841 ; *Die gute Sache der Freiheit und meine eigene Angelegenheit*, 1842 ; *Das entdeckte Christentum*, 1843 ; *Geschichte der Politik, Cultur und Aufklärung des 18ten Jarhhunderts*, 1843 and 1845 ; *Die Judenfrage*, 1843 ; *Die Fähigkeit der heutigen Juden und Christen, frei zu werden* (in *Einundzwanzig Bogen aus der Schweiz*, ed. G. Herwegh, 1843) ; *Charakteristik Ludwig Feuerbachs* (in Wigand's *Vierteljahrsschrift*, 1845, 3rd vol.) ; Articles in *Allgemeine Literatur-Zeitung*, 1844.

Bauer, Bruno and Bauer, Edgar. *Denkwürdigkeiten zur Geschichte der neueren Zeit seit der Revolution*, 7 vols., 1843.

Bauer, Edgar. *Die liberalen Bestrebungen Deutschlands*, 1843.

Bazard, Aman (1791–1832). Leader of the disciples of Saint-Simon (see Saint-Simon).

Becker, August (1814–71). Muddle-headed communist, author of several works of popularization. *Preface* to: Georg Kuhlmann—*Die neue Welt*, 1845.

Blanc, Louis (1811–82). French socialist, leader of the democratic socialist party. *Histoire de dix ans, 1830–1840*, 1841.

Bossuet, J-B. (1627–1704). French theologian and moralist, Bishop of Meaux.

*Bürgerbuch*, see *Deutsches Bürgerbuch*.

Cabet, Etienne (1788–1856). Utopian French communist, originator of abortive communist settlements in America. *Ma ligne droite ou le vrai chemin du salut pour le peuple*, 1841 ; *Voyage en Icarie*, 1842 ; Editor of *Le Populaire*.

Carnot, J-F-C. (1752–1835). Revolutionary of 1789, judge of the revolutionary tribunal.

INDEX

Chastellux, Fr. J. de. *De la Félicité publique*, 1772 (pub. anonymously).
Cherbuliez, A-E. (1797–1869). Swiss economist, follower of Sismondi.
Chevalier, Michel (1806–79). Economist, editor of various Saint-Simonist papers. *Cours d'économie politique fait au Collège de France*, 1842.
Chouroa (pseud). See Rochau.
Cobbett, William (1762–1835). English radical.
Code Napoléon. The French code of civil law, instituted by Napoleon.
Condorcet, M-J. de (1743–94). Played a prominent part in the French Revolution as a member of the Gironde. His *Esquisse d'un tableau historique des progrès de l'esprit humain*, 1794 is one of the first attempts scientifically to predict the future, and had influence on A. Comte.
Cooper, Thomas (1759–1839). American doctor, chemist and writer on economic matters. Friend of Priestley. *Lectures on the elements of political economy*, 1826.
Courrier, P-L. (1772–1824). French democrat. *Oeuvres complètes*, 4 vols., 1829–30; *Pamphlets politiques et littéraires*, 2 vols., 1831.
*Deutsches Bürgerbuch für 1845*, ed. H. Püttmann. A work to which many " true socialists " contributed (see Grün, Hess).
Edmonds, T. R. (1803–89). English follower of Robert Owen. *Practical moral and political economy* . . . 1828.
*Einundzwanzig Bogen aus der Schweiz*, 1843, ed. Georg Herwegh. A collection of articles by German radicals and Young-Hegelians (see Bruno Bauer, Hess).
*Encyclopédie, ou Dictionnaire raisonné des sciences, des arts et des métiers*, 14 vols, 1751 ff., ed. Diderot and d'Alembert. The great encyclopaedia of the French " philosophes."
Enfantin, B-P. (1796–1864). Leader of the Saint-Simonists. *Economie politique et politique* (article from *The Globe*, 1831).
Engels, Fr. (1820–95). Articles *Die Lage Englands* and *Umrisse zu einer Kritik der Nationalökonomie* in *Deutsch-Französische Jahrbücher*, 1844, ed. Ruge and Marx.
With Marx, *Die Heilige Familie oder Kritik der kritischen Kritik. Gegen Br. Bauer und Consorten*, 1845.
Feuerbach, Ludwig (1804–72). German philosopher whose criticism of religion and metaphysics was of importance in the 1840's. *Das Wesen des Christentums*, 1841; *Grundsätze der Philosophie der Zukunft*, 1843; *Vorläufige Thesen zu einer Reform der Philosophie* (in Ruge's *Anekdota*, 1843).
Fourier, Charles (1772–1837). French socialist. *Théorie des quatre mouvements*, 1808; *Théorie de l'unité universelle (Traité d'association domestique agricole)*, 1822.
Greaves, J. P. (1777–1842). English pedagogue, concerned himself with social plans for labourers on the land.

# INDEX

Grün, Karl (1817–87). " True socialist." *Die soziale Bewegung in Frankreich und Belgien*, 1845 ; *Feuerbach und die Sozialisten* (in *Deutsches Bürgerbuch für 1845*) ; Review of Mundt–*Geschichte der Gesellschaft* (in *Neue Anekdota*, 1845) ; *Politik und Sozialismus* (in *Rheinische Jahrbücher*, 1845) ; editor of *Neue Anekdota*, 1845.

Guizot, F-P-G. (1787–1874). French reactionary statesman and historian. *Histoire de la civilisation en France*, 1839.

Harney, G. J. (1817–97). Leader of the Chartists, friend of Engels, editor of the *Northern Star*.

Hegel, G. W. F. (1770–1831). *Phänomenologie des Geistes*, 1807 ; *Grundlinien der Philosophie des Rechts*, 1821 ; *Encyclopädie der philosophischen Wissenschaften im Gründrisse*, 1830 ; *Vorlesungen über die Philosophie der Geschichte*, 1837.

Heine, Heinrich (1797–1856). German poet and satirist, who contributed largely to German knowledge of social movements and ideas abroad, particularly in France. *Lyrisches Intermezzo*, 1822–3 ; *Deutschland ein Wintermärchen*, 1844 ; *Zeitgedichte*, 1844.

Hess, Moses (1812–75). One of the first Germans to popularize communistic ideas, though in a vague, often idealized form. *Die Europäische Triarchie*, 1841 ; *Philosophie der Tat* and *Socialismus und Communismus* (both in Herwegh's *Einundzwanzig Bogen*, 1843) ; *Ueber die Not in unserer Gesellschaft und deren Abhilfe*, (in *Deutsches Bürgerbuch für 1845*) ; *Ueber die sozialistische Bewegung in Deutschland* (in *Neue Anekdota*, 1845).

Hobbes, Thomas (1588–1679). English political philosopher. *Leviathan*, 1651.

Hobson, Joshua. Chartist, co-editor of the *Northern Star*.

Holbach, P-H-D. d' (1723–89). French materialist philosopher, contributor to the *Encyclopédie*. *Système de la nature ou des loix du monde physique et du monde moral*, 2 vols., 1770–1.

Holyoake, G. J. (1817–1906). A follower of Owen.

Kats, Jacob (1804–86). Flemish poet and dramatist, associated with the workers' movement.

Kuhlmann, Georg. " True socialist." *Die neue Welt oder das Reich des Geistes auf Erden, Verkündigung*, 1845 ; *Das Reich Gottes in der Wirklichkeit oder die organisierte Freiheit*, 1845.

Lamennais, F-R. de (1782–1854). Catholic socialist. *Paroles d'un croyant*, 1834.

Lerminier, J-L-E. (1803–57). French lawyer and politician, collaborated on *The Globe*. *Philosophie du droit*, 1831.

Locke, John (1632–1704). English philosopher. *On Government* and *On Civil Government*, 1690.

Mably, G-B. de (1709–85). French historian, philosopher and publicist. Wrote against private property in the interests of equality.

INDEX

Marx, Karl (1818–83). Articles *On the Jewish Question* and *A Contribution to the Critique of Hegel's Philosophy of Law* (in *Deutsch-Französische Jahrbücher*, ed. Ruge and Marx), 1844; *Die Heilige Familie*... with Engels, 1845.

Matthäi, R. "True socialist." *Sozialistische Bausteine* (in *Rheinische Jahrbücher*, 1845).

Mirabeau, E-H-R. de (1749–91). Leader during the French Revolution.

Montesquieu, C. de (1689–1755). French historian and political philosopher. *De l'Esprit des Loix*, 1748.

More, Thomas. English statesman. *Utopia*, 1516.

Morelly. Idealistic communist of the eighteenth century. *Code de la nature. Avec l'analyse raisonné du système social de Morelly par Villegardelle*, 1841. Extracts from this published in *Vorwärts*, 1844.

Morgan, J. M. (1782–1854). Follower of Owen. *Remarks on the practicability of Mr. Owen's Plan to improve the conditions of the lower classes*, 1819.

*Neue Anekdota*, 1845, edited by Karl Grün. Contains articles by "true socialists."

O'Connell, Daniel (1775–1847). Famous Irish National agitator. Called "The Liberator" for his successful management of the campaign for Catholic Emancipation (1824–1829). Bitterly opposed to "Young Ireland" Republicans and English Chartists.

Oelckers, Theodor (1816–69). German writer, translated many works from French and English. *Die Bewegung des Sozialismus und Kommunismus*, 1844.

Owen, Robert (1771–1858). English manufacturer who attempted to organize his factory on communal lines. Founder of co-operation. Utopian socialist.

Pinto, Isaak (1715–87). Dutch-Portuguese merchant and writer on economic subjects. *Lettre sur la jalousie du commerce*, 1771.

Proudhon, P-J. (1809–65). French petty-bourgeois socialist. *De la création de l'ordre dans l'humanité*, 1843; *Qu'est-ce que la propriété?* 1840; see Marx's work against Proudhon, *La misère de la philosophie*, 1847.

Pufendorf, Samuel von (1632–94). Historian of Brandenburg and political philosopher, apologist of absolutism.

Püttmann. Editor of several "true socialist" compilations. See *Deutsches Bürgerbuch, Rheinische Jahrbücher*.

Reybaud, Louis (1799–1879). French historian and economist. Edited works of Fourier. *Etudes sur les Réformateurs ou Socialistes modernes*, 3 vols, 1844.

*Rheinische Jahrbücher zur gesellschaftlichen Reform*, ed. Püttmann, 1845. Contains articles of the "true socialists" (see Grün, Matthäi, Semmig).

Rochau, A. L. von (1810–73). German liberal publicist and politician (pseudonym, Chouroa).

Rohmer, Fr. (1814–56). German radical, wrote on politics and philosophy.

INDEX 213

Rousseau, J-J. (1712–78). French political philosopher. *Du contrat social*, 1762 ; Article *Economie* in *Encyclopédie*, vol. V.

Saint-Simon, Claude-Henri de (1760–1825). Brilliant but erratic French critic of society, many of whose ideas bordered on socialism. *L'industrie, ou discussions politiques, morales et philosophiques*, 1817–8 ; *Vues sur la propriété et la législation*, 1818 ; *Lettres d'un habitant de Genève à ses concitoyens*, 1803 ; *Catéchisme politique des industriels*, 1824 ; *Nouveau Christianisme*, 1825 ; *Oeuvres*, publ. Olinde Rodrigues, 1832 ; *Vie de Saint-Simon, écrite par lui-même* (in *Oeuvres*, 1841) ; *Doctrine de Saint-Simon, Exposition*, 1828–30, ed. by his disciples on the basis of lectures by Bazard.

Say, J-B. (1767–1832). French writer on political economy.

Semmig, F. H. (1820–97). " True socialist." Article *Communismus, Socialismus, und Humanismus* (in *Rheinische Jahrbücher*, 1845, vol. I).

Sieyès, Abbé, E-J. (1748–1836). Member of the National Assembly during the French Revolution. His pamphlet, *Qu'est-ce que le tiers état ?* defined the nobility and the Church as the enemies of the people.

Sismondi, Simonde de (1773–1842). French economist whose criticism and analysis of capitalism won the esteem and attacks of Marx and Engels. *Nouveaux principes d'économie politique ou de la richesse dans ses rapports avec la population*, 1827.

Smith, Adam (1723–90). English economist, who advocated the free development of private ownership. *Wealth of Nations*, 1776.

Spence, Thomas (1750–1814). English Utopian who suggested among other things a scheme for the common ownership of the land.

Stein, Lorenz (1815–90). German writer who compiled a popular and much used account of French socialism. While in France sent reports to the Prussian Government. *Der Socialismus und Communismus des heutigen Frankreichs*, 1842.

Stirner, Max (1806–56) pseud. of J. K. Schmidt. Young-Hegelian, teacher in a Berlin girls' school. One of the first philosophical anarchists. *Der Einzige und sein Eigentum*, 1845 ; *Recensenten Stirners* (in Wigand's *Vierteljahrsschrift*, 1845, vol. 3).

Strauss D. F. (1808–74). Philosopher of religion who defined Christianity as a phase in the development of the Hegelian Idee, as a myth. *Leben Jesu*, 1835.

Thompson, William (*ca.* 1783–1833). Irish landowner, economist, socialist of Owen's school.

Turgot, A-R-J. (1727–81). French statesman and financier.

Venedey, Jakob (1805–1871). German radical publicist. Article *Credo* in *Deutsches Bürgerbuch für 1845*.

## INDEX

Villegardelle, Francois (1810–56). Disciple of Fourier. See Morelly.

*Vorwärts*. Radical paper of German émigrés in Paris, 1844–5. See Morelly.

Watts, John (1818–87). English socialist of Owen's school. Lectured in Hall of Science, Manchester. *The facts and fictions of political economists*, 1842.

Weitling, Wilhelm (1808–71). German journeyman-tailor, the first German proletarian to make a theoretical examination of communism. *Die Menschheit, wie sie ist und wie sie sein sollte*, 1838; *Garantien der Harmonie und Freiheit*, 1842.

# DIALECTICAL MATERIALISM

**LUDWIG FEUERBACH**                      **Frederick Engels**

The philosophy of Hegel and of Feuerbach. Contains the famous "Theses on Feuerbach," by Marx.

                                       Regular $1.00; Popular $0.75

**MATERIALISM AND EMPIRIO-CRITICISM**        **V. I. Lenin**

A critique of positivism and an analysis of the materialist philosophy.

                                                        $2.50

**DIALECTICAL MATERIALISM**                **V. Adoratsky**

A concise exposition, written by the director of the Marx-Engels-Lenin Institute.

                                                     Cloth 50¢

**BIOLOGY AND MARXISM**                   **Marcel Prenant**

An introduction to the problems of evolution and modern biology, this book makes clear, by practical application, the meaning of dialectical materialism and its relation to the physical sciences.

                                                       $2.50

**WHAT IS PHILOSOPHY**                    **Howard Selsam**

A Marxian introduction, designed especially for the layman.

                                        Regular $1.75; Popular $1.25

Write for a complete catalog to

## INTERNATIONAL PUBLISHERS
## 381 FOURTH AVENUE, NEW YORK CITY